Chris

W9-BFC-143

A little book,
but profound!
Much love
& gratitude
the each of you!
Curtis & Cheryl

PRAYER
THE GREATEST
POWER

Every Day Light for
Your Journey

© 2001
Text copyright by Selwyn Hughes
All rights reserved
Printed in Belgium

0–8054–2349–4

Published by Broadman & Holman Publishers, Nashville, Tennessee
Cover & Interior Design: Identity Design Inc., Dallas, Texas

Dewey Decimal Classification: 242.2
Subject Heading: DEVOTIONAL EXERCISES

Every Day Light™
CWR, Waverley Abbey House, Waverley Lane, Farnham, Surrey GU9 8EP

EDL Classic, *The Greatest Power* Text 1998 © Selwyn Hughes
Material taken from *Every Day with Jesus: Building a More Effective Prayer Life*, 1991
Revised edition in this format 1998 © Selwyn Hughes

All rights reserved, including serialization and translation. No part of this publication may be
reproduced, stored in a retrieval system, or transmitted, in any form or by any means, electronic,
mechanical, photocopying, recording, or otherwise, without the prior permission in writing of CWR.

Unless otherwise noted, Scripture quotations are from the Holy Bible,
New International Version, copyright © 1973, 1978, 1984 by International Bible Society.

SELWYN HUGHES

is the founder of CWR (Crusade for
World Revival) and the author of *Every Day
with Jesus*, a best-selling daily devotional
resource read by more than 500,000
around the world each day. He is the author
of the best-selling books *Every Day Light*,
Water for the Soul, and *Light for the Path*.
An internationally known British theologian
and commentator, Hughes lives in Farnham,
Surrey near London, England.

The Selwyn Hughes Signature Series is a collection
of elegant books each featuring daily devotionals with
Bible passages, Selwyn Hughes' own notes and
commentary, a prayer for daily meditation,
plus room for journal entries.

QUIET TIME

Lord, what a change within us, one short hour,
Spent in Thy presence will avail to make,
What heavy burdens from our bosoms take;
What parched grounds refresh as with a shower!
We kneel and all around us seems to lower,
We rise, and all the distant and the near,
Stands forth in sunny outline, brave and clear!
We kneel how weak! We rise how full of power!
Why therefore, should we do ourselves
this wrong,
Or others that we are not always strong,
That we are ever overborne with care,
That we should ever weak
Or heartless be,
Anxious or troubled, when with us is prayer,
And joy, and strength and courage
are with Thee?

Source Unknown

Signature Series

SELWYN HUGHES

PRAYER
THE GREATEST
POWER

Every Day Light for
Your Journey

BROADMAN
& HOLMAN
PUBLISHERS

NASHVILLE, TENNESSEE

WEEK 1

THE ART OF PRAYER

A quick glance at the Gospel
records will show that Jesus
constantly taught, exhorted,
encouraged and inspired
His disciples to pray.
Prayer was the breath that
He breathed, the living force
of his life, the secret of His
astonishing ministry.

— David Watson

A S A D M I N O R I T Y

"Therefore put on the full armor of God, so that when the day of evil comes, you may be able to stand your ground, and after you have done everything, to stand. Stand firm then, with the belt of truth buckled around your waist, with the breastplate of righteousness in place, and with your feet fitted with the readiness that comes from the gospel of peace. In addition to all this, take up the shield of faith, with which you can extinguish all the flaming arrows of the evil one. Take the helmet of salvation and the sword of the Spirit, which is the word of God. And pray in the Spirit on all occasions with all kinds of prayers and requests. With this in mind, be alert and always keep on praying for all the saints."

Ephesians 6:13—18

We begin today a series of meditations on what is probably the most urgent need of the Church at this present time—powerful and effective praying. The truth is that the twentieth-century church, though armed with up-to-date devices designed to make communication more effective, is nevertheless caught up in a communications breakdown. It has nothing to do with flip charts, public address systems, tape recorders or visual aids; it is a breakdown in the adequate use of the spiritual resources available to us through fervent, believing prayer. The power line between here and eternity is not being used as effectively as it might, because, quite simply, far too many Christians do not know how to pray.

The Greatest Lack

As an observer of people and their problems at first hand for over four decades, I have come to the conclusion that only a minority of Christians have an effective prayer life—ministers, missionaries, and Christian workers included. Kagawa, the famous Japanese Christian, once said to a conference of ministers on the west coast of the United States: "Your greatest lack is that you do not know how to pray." Many were incensed by the accusation, but as they continued to listen to the great man, they came to the unanimous conclusion that he was right. Many openly confessed that although they knew how to say prayers they really did not know how to pray.

"If I had one gift, and only one gift, to make to the Christian Church," said the late E. Stanley Jones, "I would offer the gift of prayer." Why this gift more than any other? Because everything follows from prayer. Everything!

Jesus, Lord and Master, how desperately I stand in need of learning to pray. Forgive me that so often I just say prayers when I ought to be praying. I sit at Your feet to listen and learn. Teach me to pray as You taught Your disciples. Amen.

"YOUR GREATEST LACK IS THAT YOU DO
NOT KNOW HOW TO PRAY."

OVERCOMING WEAKNESS

"Then Jesus told his disciples a parable to show them that they should always pray and not give up. He said, 'In a certain town there was a judge who neither feared God nor cared about men. And there was a widow in that town who kept coming to him with the plea, "Grant me justice against my adversary." For some time he refused. But finally he said to himself, "Even though I don't fear God or care about men, yet because this widow keeps bothering me, I will see that she gets justice, so that she won't eventually wear me out with her coming!"' And the Lord said, 'Listen to what the unjust judge says. And will not God bring about justice for his chosen ones, who cry out to him day and night? Will he keep putting them off?'"

Luke 18:1–7

We continue meditating on the point we made yesterday that one of the most urgent needs of the contemporary Christian Church is powerful and effective praying. Most Christians want to pray, but a busy schedule, distracting thoughts, or a hectic lifestyle undermine their best intentions. Here and there, of course, heroic souls break through the difficulties and distractions of daily living to establish for themselves a rewarding and profitable prayer life, but for most Christians it is a struggle they fail to overcome.

The Power Line

Ask anyone involved in Christian counseling why it is that we have so many spiritual casualties in the church, and they will tell you that largely it is because these people have given up at the place of prayer. If prayer fades, power fades—it is as simple as that. One Christian writer puts it like this: "When I pray, I'm like an electric bulb put into a socket—full of light and power. When I don't pray, I am like that same electric bulb disconnected from the socket—no light and no power." One of the things God longs to do with each one of us is to help us overcome our weaknesses at the place of prayer.

Some children, when they lack certain vitamins, become nervous and jumpy—even hyperactive. There are countless Christians like that—they walk through life, not with the poised sureness of spiritual mastery, but with the jumpy hysteria of starved nerves crying out for the vitamins of real life. Prayer provides us with those vitamins, for prayer is the umbilical cord between us and God. They enter our beings only when we build into our daily schedules time to communicate with God. Even a clock puts its hands together twice a day.

Gracious Father, I am so grateful that power, eternal power, is available to me—just for the taking. Help me to empty my hands of the trifling and the temporal in order to take hold of the eternal. In Christ's Name I ask it. Amen.

IF PRAYER FADES, POWER FADES.

PRAYER — THE
GREATEST POWER

"Hear my voice when I call, O LORD; be merciful to me and answer me. My heart says of you, 'Seek his face!' Your face, LORD, I will seek. Do not hide your face from me, do not turn your servant away in anger; you have been my helper. Do not reject me or forsake me, O God my Savior. Though my father and mother forsake me, the LORD will receive me. Teach me your way, O LORD; lead me in a straight path because of my oppressors. Do not turn me over to the desire of my foes, for false witnesses rise up against me, breathing out violence."

Psalm 27:7–12

William Sadler, a famous psychiatrist, said that in neglecting prayer we are "neglecting the greatest single power in the healing of disease." It is reported that he would refuse to take on a patient if that person did not believe in God, on the grounds that "it is impossible to get patients straightened out unless they have something to tie to and love beyond themselves." He went on to say: "Men and women must learn the art of prayer, for reservoirs of power are at our disposal if we can learn this art."

The Art of Prayer

I have a slight problem with that last statement of Sadler as it seems to suggest that the reason why we must learn the art of prayer is that we might get its benefits, and while this is entirely true, it is not the entire truth. The primary reason why we must learn the art of prayer is in order to know God better. It is also true that the better we know God, the better we will function. But we must be careful to get the priorities in the right order.

The main point I want to pick up in today's meditation is that prayer is not simply an exercise, but it is an art. Proficiency in the art depends on how much we are prepared to engage in its exercise. Many Christians expect results without any practice or exercise. We would regard a person as very foolish who stepped up to a musical instrument only occasionally, expecting to tune into music and become the instrument of music without training and practice. If we spent half the time learning the art of prayer that we spend learning any other art, we would get ten times the results.

O Father, help me learn the greatest of all arts—the art of praying. Give me the mind to pray, the love to pray, the will to pray. Let prayer be the aroma of every act, the atmosphere of every thought. Indeed, let it be my native air. Amen.

WE MUST LEARN THE ART OF PRAYER IN ORDER TO KNOW GOD BETTER.

ANYONE CAN LEARN

"Blessed is he whose transgressions are forgiven, whose sins are covered. Blessed is the man whose sin the LORD does not count against him and in whose spirit is no deceit. When I kept silent, my bones wasted away through my groaning all day long. For day and night your hand was heavy upon me; my strength was sapped as in the heat of summer. Then I acknowledged my sin to you and did not cover up my iniquity. I said, 'I will confess my transgressions to the LORD'— and you forgave the guilt of my sin. Therefore let everyone who is godly pray to you while you may be found; surely when the mighty waters rise, they will not reach him. You are my hiding place; you will protect me from trouble and surround me with songs of deliverance."

Psalm 32:1–7

We spend another day enlarging on the point that prayer is an art. We live, as someone has said, "in an open universe," meaning that anything that is right is possible, if we will obey God's laws of accomplishment and relate ourselves to them. Just as, when God made the world, He left certain things dependent on the action of our wills—some gardens, for example, would not look in the perfect condition that they do without care and cultivation—so He has left certain things dependent upon prayer. To put it bluntly—certain things will never happen unless we pray.

Prayer Needs Practice

Someone shared with me the other day the story of her five-year-old son who, having heard the tune "God Save the Queen" being played on a harmonica in the department store they were visiting, pleaded with his mother to buy him one. She did and when he got home, the first thing he did was take out the instrument and blow into it. After a while he burst into tears and threw the instrument contemptuously aside, crying, "There is no 'God Save the Queen' in this harmonica!" We are just as foolish if we believe we can get ready-made results without the practice of prayer.

Now be careful you don't misunderstand what I am saying. I am not saying that whenever we find ourselves in an emergency, a quick telegram to heaven does not bring results. It most certainly does. God is quick and eager to respond to the faintest cry of one of His desperate children. What I am saying is this—to achieve power in prayer, to draw upon its immense potential, and to make use of all its awesome benefits, one has to put its principles into practice and give time to learning the art.

Father, I confess that my feet stumble on
the path of prayer. I am learning to walk, but there
are hard places. Teach me how to apply myself to
prayer that I might become proficient in the art.
In Jesus' name I ask it. Amen.

TO ACHIEVE POWER IN PRAYER ONE HAS TO PUT PRINCIPLES
INTO PRACTICE.

15

AN OPEN UNIVERSE

"When Solomon had finished the temple of the LORD and the royal palace, and had succeeded in carrying out all he had in mind to do in the temple of the LORD and in his own palace, the LORD appeared to him at night and said: 'I have heard your prayer and have chosen this place for myself as a temple for sacrifices. When I shut up the heavens so that there is no rain, or command locusts to devour the land or send a plague among my people, if my people, who are called by my name, will humble themselves and pray and seek my face and turn from their wicked ways, then will I hear from heaven and will forgive their sin and will heal their land.'"

2 Chronicles 7:11–14

We turn now to focus on some of the questions that people raise when confronted with the challenge to pray. We begin with what is probably the biggest question of all: If God is all-knowing, He doesn't need us to voice our concern; and if He is all-loving, then He will see that we have our need without the necessity of dragging it out of Him through persevering prayer. So why pray?

The question, of course, represents a befuddled and confused view of prayer. It is true that because God loves us He orders and arranges events in our lives that work for good whether we pray or not, but there are vast areas of life where things will not just happen—unless we pray. Let it stagger you if you will, but the truth is that God has given us the freedom to affect the course of some events in His universe by our prayers.

The Outcome of Prayer

C. S. Lewis once compared history to a play where the scenery and general outline are fixed by the playwright but certain things are left for the actors and actresses to improvise on. The illustration has some weaknesses, but in general it represents a fair picture of how God has set up the universe. God has foreordained certain things to happen, of course, but above and beyond that there are things which will come to pass only if we pray.

Revival is one of those things. Our text for today makes that point perfectly clear. Note the word *if.* "If my people . . . will humble themselves and pray." Even a child knows that the word *if* is a word of condition. God is saying, "If you pray then I will hear." Can anything be more clear? As Tennyson put it: "More things are wrought by prayer than this world dreams of."

Gracious and loving Father, I see that some things just won't get done unless I pray. Help me ponder this truth until it drives me to my knees to cooperate with You in bringing Your purposes to pass in this world. In Jesus' Name. Amen.

"MORE THINGS ARE WROUGHT BY PRAYER THAN THIS WORLD DREAMS OF."

W I D E L Y   O P E N E D

T O   H E A V E N

"Peter was kept in prison, but the church was earnestly praying to God for him. The night before Herod was to bring him to trial, Peter was sleeping between two soldiers, bound with two chains, and sentries stood guard at the entrance. Suddenly an angel of the Lord appeared and a light shone in the cell. He struck Peter on the side and woke him up. 'Quick, get up!' he said, and the chains fell off Peter's wrists. Then the angel said to him, 'Put on your clothes and sandals.' And Peter did so. 'Wrap your cloak around you and follow me,' the angel told him. Peter followed him out of the prison, but he had no idea that what the angel was doing was really happening; he thought he was seeing a vision."

Acts 12:5–9

Another question that often comes up when the subject of prayer is raised is this: If prayer is so powerful, why hasn't it produced greater changes than we are presently seeing in the affairs of men and women? There are two clear answers to this. The first I will deal with today and the second tomorrow.

The first reason, I suggest, why we do not see greater changes for good in the world is because not enough prayer is being made. I once heard the great Methodist preacher, the late W. E. Sangster, say that God pours His redemptive power into the world through the funnel of His people's prayers. The more prayer that is made, the more power that gets through and in some situations in this world

God does not move except in response to the concerted prayers of His people.

Effective Prayer

Sangster made the point, also, that there is a great difference between saying prayers and praying. Every Sunday God's people meet in church and go through different forms of praying. Some use printed prayers, some memorize prayers and say them or sing them in concert with others. And some pray extemporaneous prayers. Saying prayers is fine, but we must see that this is simply one level of praying. The kind of praying that reaches out and makes an impact upon the world of men and women is the fervent, believing, intercessory prayer that we will come to and define a little later. I am bold to say that when it comes to intercessory prayer, not enough of it is being made. We say prayers but we are not praying.

Prayer at its best opens earth to heaven. Just think—what would happen if through prayer this earth were widely opened to heaven?

O Father, I see that some of the problems we face in our world are there because we, Your people, have not prayed enough. Forgive us that so often we simply say prayers when we ought to be praying. Teach us the art of intercession. In Jesus' Name. Amen.

PRAYER AT ITS BEST OPENS EARTH TO HEAVEN.

QUALITY PRAYER

"What causes fights and quarrels among you? Don't they come from your desires that battle within you? You want something but don't get it. You kill and covet, but you cannot have what you want. You quarrel and fight. You do not have, because you do not ask God. When you ask, you do not receive, because you ask with wrong motives, that you may spend what you get on your pleasures."

James 4:1–3

We look now at another answer to the question we raised yesterday: If prayer is so powerful, why hasn't it produced greater changes in the affairs of men and women than we are presently seeing? A second answer is this: The prayers we offer lack quality and depth. When we pause to examine our prayer life, we find that so much of it is shot through with selfishness and egocentricity. We are like the young woman who continually prayed in public that God would give her a husband. When asked by her minister to keep that kind of prayer for her private devotions, she got up in the next prayer meeting and prayed: "Lord, please give my mother a son-in-law." Selfish praying consists of relating everything to ourselves, and there is far too much of that in our public and private petitions.

Conversation with the Creator

Added to selfishness and egocentricity is the problem of praying merely from a sense of duty rather than experiencing in prayer a sense of wondrous relationship with God. Some talk to the Almighty as if they are talking into a tape recorder and have no feeling of awe and wonder that they are actually conversing with the living God. Prayer is talking, listening, and conversing with the great God of the universe—a privilege accorded to those who are His redeemed children.

If prayer is conversation, then when we pray we ought to hear more than our own voice; we ought to hear His voice also. When did you last hear God whisper something to you as you were at prayer? When did you last expect Him to say something? No one can say that prayer fails until they are sure that it is of the quality that heaven demands.

Father, help me understand that You are
not so much interested in the arithmetic of my
prayers—how many there are; or the oratory of
my prayers—how eloquent they are; but in
the sincerity of my prayers—how real they are.
Help me pray, dear Lord. Amen.

PRAYER IS TALKING, LISTENING, AND CONVERSING WITH
THE GREAT GOD OF THE UNIVERSE.

Is prayer

your

steering wheel

or your

spare tire?

—Corrie Ten Boom

_____

_____

_____

_____

_____

_____

_____

_____

_____

_____

_____

_____

_____

_____

_____

_____

_____

_____

_____

_____

_____

WEEK 2

WHAT IS PRAYER?

Prayer is the sum of
our relationship with God.
We are what we pray.
The degree of our faith
is a degree of our prayer.
Our ability to love
is our ability to pray.

— Carlo Carretto

THE GREAT COOPERATION

"Blessed is the man who makes the LORD his trust, who does not look to the proud, to those who turn aside to false gods. Many, O LORD my God, are the wonders you have done. The things you planned for us no one can recount to you; were I to speak and tell of them, they would be too many to declare. Sacrifice and offering you did not desire, but my ears you have pierced; burnt offerings and sin offerings you did not require. Then I said, 'Here I am, I have come—it is written about me in the scroll. To do your will, O my God, is my desire; your law is within my heart.'"

Psalm 40:4–8

Now that we have established the fact that prayer is a necessity and not just a luxury in the Christian life, we are ready to face the question: What exactly is prayer? First, prayer is cooperation with God. In prayer you align your will, your desires, your life to God. You and God become one on the matter of your life plans, your life goals and your life desires, and you proceed to work them out together. When your desires are one, then your decisions will be one, and when your decisions are one, your power is one.

If we don't start with the understanding that prayer is cooperation with God, then we will finish up trying to get God to do our will instead of surrendering to His will.

It is important to recognize, of course, that the will is not a separate portion of us—the will does not function in a vacuum—but is the expression of the inner self. Behind our will is our whole nature, and what prayer does is align the whole of our self, the whole of our nature, to the will of God.

Attuned to God

In this respect I often think of prayer as attuning. Just as when a note on a well-tuned piano is struck the corresponding note on a well-tuned violin vibrates in unison, so when God strikes certain notes in His nature we find our heartstrings vibrating in unison. That is what prayer achieves—it sensitizes us to the will and purpose of God. A withholding of consent and cooperation can tie God's hands, but the giving of consent and the giving of cooperation free God's hands so that all things are made possible.

Note, God will not force us to do this. He will not break down our personalities in order to obtain our consent. He simply stands and waits.

O Father, You have given Yourself to me;
now help me to give myself to You. Help me to
know You so intimately that when Your heart
vibrates there will be an answering vibration in me.
I ask this in Jesus' Name. Amen.

IN PRAYER YOU ALIGN YOUR WILL, YOUR DESIRES,
YOUR LIFE TO GOD.

"BY SMALL ACCOMPLISHING GREAT"

"The law is only a shadow of the good things that are coming—not the realities themselves. For this reason it can never, by the same sacrifices repeated endlessly year after year, make perfect those who draw near to worship. If it could, would they not have stopped being offered? For the worshipers would have been cleansed once for all, and would no longer have felt guilty for their sins. But those sacrifices are an annual reminder of sins, because it is impossible for the blood of bulls and goats to take away sins. Therefore, when Christ came into the world, he said: 'Sacrifice and offering you did not desire, but a body you prepared for me; with burnt offerings and sin offerings you were not pleased. Then I said, "Here I am—it is written about me in the scroll—I have come to do your will, O God."'"

Hebrews 10:1–7

We continue with the thought that prayer is cooperation with God. We must have done with the idea that prayer is bending God's will to our will; it is a bringing of our will into conformity with His will so that His will may work in and through us. When you are in a small boat and you throw out a boat hook to catch hold of the shore, do you pull the shore to yourself or do you pull yourself to the shore?

Milton used the phrase, "by small accomplishing great things." We do just that when we cooperate with God in prayer. A little boy once gave his five loaves and two fishes to Jesus—he cooperated with Jesus in the feeding of the multitude. How his eyes must have bulged and his heart danced as he saw his little become big, the insufficient become adequate. When we cooperate with God in His plans—and we are more likely to do that following prayer—then He cooperates with us in His power.

Perfect Alignment

Be careful with this next statement because it can easily be misinterpreted—when we do what He says, then He will do what we say. A translation of John 15:7 reads thus: "If you live your life in me, and my words live in your hearts, you can ask for whatever you like and it will come true for you" (Phillips). Somebody has said concerning prayer: "It is the purest exercise of the faculties God has given us—an exercise that links our faculties with our Maker in order to work out His intentions." I like that definition because in a single sentence it clarifies for me what prayer is all about—prayer is aligning ourselves with the purposes of God. It enables us to do what we were designed to do—cooperate with the Eternal.

Father, help me not to ask for tasks equal to my power, but power equal to my tasks. Show me how cooperation with You in prayer throws open infinite possibilities. And help me walk in. In Jesus' Name I ask it. Amen.

WHEN WE COOPERATE WITH GOD IN HIS PLANS, THEN HE COOPERATES WITH US IN HIS POWER.

THE WAY TO LIFE

"Then he said to them all: 'If anyone would come after me, he must deny himself and take up his cross daily and follow me. For whoever wants to save his life will lose it, but whoever loses his life for me will save it. What good is it for a man to gain the whole world, and yet lose or forfeit his very self? If anyone is ashamed of me and my words, the Son of Man will be ashamed of him when he comes in his glory and in the glory of the Father and of the holy angels. I tell you the truth, some who are standing here will not taste death before they see the kingdom of God.'"

Luke 9:23–27

We said yesterday that prayer is cooperation with God. However, we would have only a limited view of prayer if we were to stay with that one definition. To cooperate fully with God means totally to surrender the self. Second, then, prayer is surrender—the surrendering of all we are in order to receive all that is an offer from the divine hands.

A Controlling Purpose

I have found over the years that some Christians don't like the word *surrender;* it conjures up in their minds a vision of becoming a non-person, a cipher, mushy and meaningless. But nothing could be further from the truth. Surrendering to God does not produce a meaningless self but an alert self:

a self no longer eager for its own way but for the divine way; a self that, knowing its place as second, is eager to serve the First. A surrendered self is not pulp; it is a person, but a person with a controlling purpose, which is to follow the Person who is above all persons—wherever He may lead.

A woman describing her prayer life to me put it like this: "I just go limp in His presence and give God time, then wait for His loving counsel to come through." That is what I mean by surrender: "giving God time for His loving counsel to come through." Note in these words the thought both of time and receptivity. Time alone would not be enough, there must also be alert receptivity. I am convinced that God comes into the core of our beings along the pathway of surrender and receptivity. You cannot inscribe anything on a tense, self-absorbed mind. Thus, all fears must be surrendered, and all self-will, so that He may imprint His directions and desires on the soul.

O God, I throw open every pore of my being to You this day. Show me that in yielding to You I am not losing my life but finding it. It sounds at first like the way to death, but I see it is the way to life. Help me, in Jesus' Name. Amen.

PRAYER IS SURRENDER.

WE SHARE THE THRONE!

"Suppose one of you wants to build a tower. Will he not first sit down and estimate the cost to see if he has enough money to complete it? For if he lays the foundation and is not able to finish it, everyone who sees it will ridicule him, saying, 'This fellow began to build and was not able to finish.' Or suppose a king is about to go to war against another king. Will he not first sit down and consider whether he is able with ten thousand men to oppose the one coming against him with twenty thousand? If he is not able, he will send a delegation while the other is still a long way off and will ask for terms of peace. In the same way, any of you who does not give up everything he has cannot be my disciple."

Luke 14:28–33

We continue looking at prayer as surrender—a surrender of our purposes, plans, will, and desires into the hands of God. But let me once again make the point I touched on yesterday—surrender does not imply weak negativism. Prayer is like the wire that surrenders to the dynamo, the flower to the sun, the student to the teacher. The Gulf Stream will flow through a drinking straw, provided the straw is aligned to the Gulf Stream and is not blocked in any way. You, as an individual, surrender to God in prayer, and then God gives Himself to you.

I almost said, "surrenders" to you, but I thought I might be misunderstood. Yet that is what happens—we surrender to Him, and He surrenders to us. That does not mean that we can do what we like with God and twist Him around our little finger. When we are surrendered to Him, then we will only want the things He wants, and we will ask for nothing that is not in accord with His will.

Power-Sharing

There is a thrilling verse in Revelation 3:21 that says, "To him who overcomes, I will give the right to sit with me on my throne, just as I overcame and sat down with my Father on his throne." Ever thought about that? Here is Christ, the Son of God, telling poor mortals that just as He sat down with His Father on the throne, so we are to sit with Him on the throne: as . . . so. Of course, this verse is referring to something that is yet to happen, but in one sense it happens right now. When we surrender to Him and cooperate with Him, then we share the ideas and powers which rule the universe. We share His throne! We are part of the ruling ideas and powers which guide and govern the universe.

Lord Jesus, You called me to a cross but lo, as I took it, it turned out to be a throne. I share that throne because it is a throne of grace. Only grace would share its power. I am so deeply, deeply thankful. Amen.

WHEN WE ARE SURRENDERED TO GOD, WE WILL WANT ONLY THE THINGS HE WANTS.

TAKING AND UNDERTAKING

"Very early in the morning, while it was still dark, Jesus got up, left the house and went off to a solitary place, where he prayed. Simon and his companions went to look for him, and when they found him, they exclaimed: 'Everyone is looking for you!' Jesus replied, 'Let us go somewhere else—to the nearby villages—so I can preach there also. That is why I have come.' So he traveled throughout Galilee, preaching in their synagogues and driving out demons."

Mark 1:35–39

Today we look at yet another aspect of prayer—creativity. If prayer were only surrender, it would leave us leaning too much toward the passive side. We would take without undertaking. The taking from God must produce an undertaking for God—we become minicreators. In prayer our lesser life touches the divine life, and we receive a quickening. We become alive—alive to the fingertips.

Divine Direction

I chose the passage before us today because it illustrates the point I am attempting to make—that from the place of prayer Jesus came forth with a creative mission—"Let us go into the next towns, that I may preach . . ." (v. 38 NKJV).

His praying was preaching—preaching in incubation. The praying produced in Him a clear direction, and His surrender turned into a response. "The most active persons in the world," said E. Stanley Jones, "are the people who become inactive in the Silence." What did he mean? He meant, I think, that the people who take time to pray learn to live in the passive voice that they might live more effectively in the active voice. The poised, prayerful heart is sure of its directions, sure of its resources and moves from task to task with calm confidence.

A theological student told of the tremendous effect upon him of the words of a great preacher who stood up in the morning assembly and prayed, "O God, may we wake up to Jesus!" Prayer does just that—it wakes us up to Jesus. It gives us His awareness, His creativity, His energy. In the Garden of Gethsemane, following one of the most powerful prayer moments of His life, our Lord said, "Rise, let us be going" (Matt. 26:46 NKJV).

O God, wake me up to Jesus. Give me His passion for prayer and His passion for people. May my needs give me to You and the needs of others give me to them. Through prayer I discover a working force; help me to utilize it. Amen.

PRAYER WAKES US UP TO JESUS.

" T H E N   Y O U
B E   H I S   H A N D S "

"You have heard of my previous way of life in Judaism, how intensely I persecuted the church of God and tried to destroy it. I was advancing in Judaism beyond many Jews of my own age and was extremely zealous for the traditions of my fathers. But when God, who set me apart from birth and called me by his grace, was pleased to reveal his Son in me so that I might preach him among the Gentiles, I did not consult any man, nor did I go up to Jerusalem to see those who were apostles before I was, but I went immediately into Arabia and later returned to Damascus."

Galatians 1:13–17

We continue with the thought that prayer is creativity. When we cooperate with God in prayer and surrender to Him, then we extend ourselves through Him. In the central church in Copenhagen there is a figure of Christ, created by Thorwaldson, that has brought tears to the eyes of many visitors. The story is told of a little Danish girl who once found a small replica of Thorwaldson's Christ in an abandoned house. She brought it to her father and said: "But it has no hands; they have been broken off." The father replied, "Then you be His hands." The little girl thought long and hard about that and during her teenage years surrendered her life to Christ and became a missionary to India. Her missionary work was categorized by her peers as "unusual and creative." She prayed a lot, and out of her prayer life came a creativity that marked her out as equal to her colleagues but different.

Becoming a Boon

Cooperation and surrender in prayer produced creativity—it always does. You see, prayer is not begging for boons; it is becoming a boon—to yourself and to others. Prayer adds a plus to all thinking and all living. Through prayer we become extensions of the Incarnation—we enable the creative Christ to continue His creative ministry in and through our surrendered lives. Our Lord extends His personality through us and in doing so extends our personalities. The Creator stimulates us into creativity.

By cooperation and surrender in prayer, you can be His hands with which He touches others, His feet through which He seeks out others, His heart through which He loves others. You!

O Father, I sense You are offering me breathtaking power. Help me to surrender to it so that I may then rise to it. Make me an extension of Your Incarnation in every situation in which I find myself this day. In Jesus' Name. Amen.

YOU CAN BE HIS HANDS . . . HIS FEET . . . HIS HEART.

"GOD'S HAND ON YOUR SHOULDER"

"Do you not know? Have you not heard? The LORD is the everlasting God, the Creator of the ends of the earth. He will not grow tired or weary, and his understanding no one can fathom. He gives strength to the weary and increases the power of the weak. Even youths grow tired and weary, and young men stumble and fall; but those who hope in the LORD will renew their strength. They will soar on wings like eagles; they will run and not grow weary, they will walk and not be faint."

Isaiah 40:28–31

I feel compelled to spend one more day looking at prayer as creativity. Out of the quietness with God, power is generated that turns the spiritual machinery of our lives. Prayer is not an end in itself: it is a means to an end. When we pray, we begin to feel the sense of being sent, that the divine creative compulsion is upon us. As one young Christian put it, "When you pray you no longer have a chip on your shoulder you have a hand on your shoulder—God's hand."

A Sense of Mission

Is it surprising that we come from the place of prayer with a sense of creativity? Not when we realize that when we pray we are putting our beings at the disposal of God, and that He, in turn, is touching and anointing us so that a sense of mission is put into all our faculties. We consecrate our powers to Him, and He consecrates our beings and tunes us in readiness for whatever service He proposes. Prayer that keeps us focused only on ourselves is not true prayer, for one of the ends of prayer is to provide us with the energy and power we need to face whatever task God has put ahead of us and to perform it creatively. We pray, but in addition to the work of prayer, there is further work to be done—creative work for our Master.

I love the following lines that I came across many years ago and recorded in my notes (I regret I don't know the author):

You must use your hands while praying, though,
If an answer you would get;
For prayer-worn knees and a rusty hoe
Never raised a big crop yet.

O God, I consecrate all my energies and all my powers to You, that You, in turn, may consecrate them to Your purposes and Your plans. Teach me how to wait before You in prayer and then go forth from there with Your hand upon my shoulder. In Jesus' Name. Amen.

PRAYER IS NOT AN END IN ITSELF: IT IS A MEANS TO AN END.

Prayer is not a lovely sedan for a sight-seeing trip around the city. Prayer is a truck that goes straight to the warehouse, backs up, loads, comes home with the goods.

—John R. Rice

WEEK 3

PRAYER FOR LIFE

Prayer is a matchless
opportunity. Through prayer,
people, things, problems
and relationships can be
transformed. Prayer has
infinite power—because it
is directed to an infinitely
powerful God.

— Basilea Schlink

B E C O M I N G
G O D - I N F U S E D

"For this reason I kneel before the Father, from whom his whole family in heaven and on earth derives its name. I pray that out of his glorious riches he may strengthen you with power through his Spirit in your inner being, so that Christ may dwell in your hearts through faith. And I pray that you, being rooted and established in love, may have power, together with all the saints, to grasp how wide and long and high and deep is the love of Christ, and to know this love that surpasses knowledge—that you may be filled to the measure of all the fullness of God."

Ephesians 3:14—19

Prayer, as we are seeing, has many facets. We have looked at three—cooperation, surrender and creativity—now we look at a fourth—transfusion. When we pray, a transfusion of divine life enters into our souls; we experience a renewal, a renewal of resources. Like old-fashioned watches, life has a tendency to run down. It needs rewinding. Prayer does just that—it rewinds the spring of life. Instead of turning to prayer, many tinker with the hands and try to push them around—and finish up in breakdown or burnout.

Prayer brings resources that are not found anywhere else in the world. In the college where I was trained for the ministry, there was a prayer room with this sign on the door: "It is so easy to get lost in this world; come on in and find yourself." In the years I spent preparing for the ministry, I got lost many times—lost in terms of my direction—but I would go into the prayer room, prostrate myself before God, and find my way again—invariably.

A Life Transfusion

This morning in my daily quiet time my eyes fell on this passage: "And great multitudes came together to hear, and to be healed by him of their infirmities. So He Himself often withdrew into the wilderness and prayed" (Luke 5:15–16 NKJV). He ran away from the crowds—to pray. We run after the crowds—and don't pray. Some preachers are more crowd-conscious than prayer-conscious, but not Jesus. Then, when the crowds got to Him, He was ready because He had replenished His resources by prayer. We read: "the power of the Lord was present to heal" (Luke 5:17 NKJV). Prayer is a lift-up with no let-down. In waiting before God you have a life transfusion. You become God-infused.

O God, as I wait before You in prayer this day, give me a transfusion of Your life. Inject Your power into my withered veins so that I shall live abundantly, vibrantly, vitally. In Jesus' Name. Amen.

PRAYER REWINDS THE SPRING OF LIFE.

THE DEEPEST EDUCATION

"I am the true vine, and my Father is the gardener. He cuts off every branch in me that bears no fruit, while every branch that does bear fruit he prunes so that it will be even more fruitful. You are already clean because of the word I have spoken to you. Remain in me, and I will remain in you. No branch can bear fruit by itself; it must remain in the vine. Neither can you bear fruit unless you remain in me. I am the vine; you are the branches. If a man remains in me and I in him, he will bear much fruit; apart from me you can do nothing."

John 15:1–5

A fifth aspect of prayer is this—revision. Someone said, "A revised version of your life is put out every time you pray, really pray." When you sit in silence before God and wait for Him to speak to you, then you bring more and more areas of your life under His control, more and more powers are put at your disposal, and your being is more and more closely aligned to the being of God.

In a debate some time ago on the subject of education I heard a speaker say, "The whole purpose of education is change—change from ignorance to knowledge, change from not knowing to knowing." If that is true, I said to myself, then prayer is life's deepest education, for in prayer we are being educated at the place that counts—the spirit.

Day by day, dear Lord,
Of Thee three things I pray:
To see Thee more clearly,
To love Thee more dearly,
To follow Thee more nearly,
Day by day.

Prayer Prunes

Because prayer involves revision, a certain amount of pruning has to go on. Many of us find that our lives are overgrown with the unimportant. We are busy but are doing nothing. Prayer brings the important to the center of consciousness and pushes the unimportant to the edges. In prayer we give God time to prune the branches of our lives and cut away those sucker branches that sap the life of the branch—suckers that bear no fruit and keep the branch from bearing fruit. Prayer prunes our persons and our purposes.

O God, forgive me that I give so much time
to the unimportant and so little time to the
important. My life needs to be revised. Teach me
to pray, and out of my prayer life bring forth
a new and revised edition. In Jesus' Name. Amen.

"A REVISED VERSION OF YOUR LIFE IS PUT OUT
EVERY TIME YOU PRAY."

ONE LOOK AT JESUS

"The Lord said to Ananias, 'Go! This man is my chosen instrument to carry my name before the Gentiles and their kings and before the people of Israel. I will show him how much he must suffer for my name.' Then Ananias went to the house and entered it. Placing his hands on Saul, he said, 'Brother Saul, the Lord—Jesus, who appeared to you on the road as you were coming here—has sent me so that you may see again and be filled with the Holy Spirit.' Immediately, something like scales fell from Saul's eyes, and he could see again. He got up and was baptized, and after taking some food, he regained his strength."

Acts 9:15—19

We continue with the thought that prayer is revision. As he worked, a famous artist kept beside him a collection of precious stones of many colors. When asked why, he replied: "I find it helpful from time to time to wash out my eyes in the colors of nature." The colors helped to clarify and sharpen his own sense of color. This is what we do when we pray—we look at Jesus and His colors clarify our colors. Black is never grey in His presence, and white is never cream. He holds within Himself the power for giving us clear distinctions about everything, whether moral or general. And when we pray, His influence gets to work on us.

Jesus' Purity

A missionary, who worked many years in the slum areas of London, tried to get a group of children to clean themselves up. They didn't respond until the missionary went to another part of London and brought a child with clean clothes and a clean face. Then they went off one by one and washed their faces. A Christian young man I knew who was gripped by the smoking habit and unable to give it up told me that one day he sat with a Christian friend who so radiated Christ that he took out his cigarettes, threw them away, and never smoked again. I know something of what that young man spoke about. Often when I look into the face of Jesus, I want to throw something away— a wrong attitude, a harbored resentment, a foolish thought. Jesus' purity encourages purity in me.

This is what I meant when I said yesterday that a revised version of our life is put out every time we pray. So take hold of this truth again—prayer is revision. It prunes our purposes, our plans, and our person.

O Jesus, my Lord and Master, I look into Your face, and I go away feeling as though I want to throw away something. I want to empty my hands so that I may more fully take hold of the eternally worthwhile. Amen.

WHEN WE PRAY, WE LOOK AT JESUS—AND HIS COLORS CLARIFY OUR COLORS.

THE ONE TRUE REALITY

"I am coming to you now, but I say these things while I am still in the world, so that they may have the full measure of my joy within them. I have given them your word and the world has hated them, for they are not of the world any more than I am of the world. My prayer is not that you take them out of the world but that you protect them from the evil one. They are not of the world, even as I am not of it. Sanctify them by the truth; your word is truth. As you sent me into the world, I have sent them into the world. For them I sanctify myself, that they too may be truly sanctified."

John 17:13–19

Prayer is all the things we have been discussing, but it is also much more. Another aspect of prayer is this—being in touch with reality. There are some who feel that prayer is a good spiritual exercise, and they put it in the same category as autosuggestion. Personally, I would find it difficult to give myself to prayer if I believed that all I was doing was giving myself a psychological shot in the arm. Autosuggestion may have benefits, but when it comes to coping with life, I want to know that I am in touch with God's plans and purposes for my being. I most certainly do not want to live in a fool's paradise. I want to know I am in touch with truth and reality.

The Need for Objectivity

In my teenage years I studied very closely the whole subject of autosuggestion in order to counter the views of my father, who for a few months became deeply preoccupied with it. He had a stomach ulcer and used to go around the house repeating the famous phrase of Emille Coue: "Every day, in every way, I am getting better and better." Actually, the reverse happened, and he got worse and worse. Eventually, at the insistence of my mother and me, he sought proper medical attention and then, having dealt with the situation more realistically, found the help and care he needed.

Sin has so damaged the inner fabric of our beings that we cannot hope to build our lives on what we find within. We need an objectivity that is reliable and verifiable. Jesus is that objectivity. I love what one philosopher said about Him: "Reality, whose other name is Jesus." Something happens whenever we bow our knees or lift up our hearts in prayer—something very real.

Lord Jesus Christ, You are the finest and the most real character who ever lived—and yet You prayed. Remind me every time I lift my heart to You in prayer that I am in touch with the one true reality. For Your own dear Name's sake. Amen.

PRAYER IS BEING IN TOUCH WITH REALITY.

NOT AUTOSUGGESTION
BUT OTHER-SUGGESTION

"The righteous cry out, and the LORD hears them; he delivers them from all their troubles. The LORD is close to the brokenhearted and saves those who are crushed in spirit. A righteous man may have many troubles, but the LORD delivers him from them all; he protects all his bones, not one of them will be broken. Evil will slay the wicked; the foes of the righteous will be condemned. The LORD redeems his servants; no one will be consumed who takes refuge in him."

Psalm 34:17–22

We continue with the thought that prayer is being in touch with reality and not just simply autosuggestion. How many times have we heard atheistic or agnostic writers ridicule prayer by saying it is simply "wishful thinking" or "an echo of your own voice"? Suppose it were autosuggestion, even on that level it would be a healthy thing. Better to suggest to yourself the highest than the lowest. Those who know what prayer is all about, however, would define prayer not as autosuggestion but Other-suggestion—the Other being God. Prayer would never have survived if it were nothing but autosuggestion, with no voice answering our voice, no heart answering our heart.

The God Who Answers

The only competent witnesses to the power of prayer are those who use it. Listen to how one poet puts it:

Whoso has felt the Spirit of the Highest
Cannot confound nor doubt him nor deny,
Yea, with one voice, O world, though thou deniest
Stand thou on this side, for on this am I!

If a flower could believe, do you think it would believe that the sun is only the projection of itself? Could a wire believe that the energy that pulses through it comes from within and not from the power source? In true prayer there is a wondrous sense of otherness that can only be described as the presence of the living God. Something—no, Someone—answers, and answers in terms of release, power, insight, vitality, and heightened accomplishment. Is this an illusion?

Father, it cannot be, for out of nothing, nothing can come. I kneel and all around is Your power, Your presence, Your peace. Teach me more, dear Lord, of the power that flows toward me in prayer. I would live—and live abundantly. Amen.

IN TRUE PRAYER THERE IS A WONDROUS
SENSE OF OTHERNESS.

SUBCONSCIOUS COMMUNION

"I have seen you in the sanctuary and beheld your power and your glory. Because your love is better than life, my lips will glorify you. I will praise you as long as I live, and in your name I will lift up my hands. My soul will be satisfied as with the richest of foods; with singing lips my mouth will praise you. On my bed I remember you; I think of you through the watches of the night. Because you are my help, I sing in the shadow of your wings. my soul clings to you; your right hand upholds me."

Psalm 63:2–8

Another aspect of prayer is this—communion. Those who see prayer as simply asking for things struggle to understand this aspect of the devotional life. I love the story of the little boy who came into his father's study. When asked what he wanted, he replied, "Nothing. I just want to be with you."

There are times in prayer when one's own wants and needs drop away and the focus is on contemplating Him. A young Christian tells how, in the early days of his Christian experience, the phrase that he most used in his prayer life was this: "Lord, You've got me." In later years, however, it changed to this: "Lord, I love You." What had happened? As he had grown in prayer, the focus had changed from himself to Christ. He knew what it was to experience communion.

Words of Love

A famous missionary tells how every night before he goes to sleep he focuses on the phrase: "I love You, Lord." And the moment he wakes up he finds himself saying the same words. He claims his subconscious has been repeating them through the night hours. It is a fact that the subconscious holds on to the last thought of the conscious mind as we go to sleep and then delivers it back to us when we awake. The subconscious never sleeps: it is active when we are inactive, alert when we are asleep. And it will work on anything we choose to hand over to it in the moments when we fall asleep. If our last thought at night is one of worry and concern, our subconscious will spend the night worrying for us. Then we will wake up tired and irritable. As you go to sleep, learn to say in a meaningful way: "I love You, Lord," and let your mind enjoy subconscious communion with God.

O Father, help me see that prayer is more than just petitioning You for things, but a way in which I can just enjoy You and You enjoy me. In Jesus' Name I pray. Amen.

AS ONE GROWS IN PRAYER, THE FOCUS CHANGES FROM ONESELF TO CHRIST.

COMMUNION MOMENT

"My soul finds rest in God alone; my salvation comes from him. He alone is my rock and my salvation; he is my fortress, I will never be shaken. How long will you assault a man? Would all of you throw him down—this leaning wall, this tottering fence? They fully intend to topple him from his lofty place; they take delight in lies. With their mouths they bless, but in their hearts they curse. Find rest, O my soul, in God alone; my hope comes from him. He alone is my rock and my salvation; he is my fortress, I will not be shaken."

Psalm 62:1–6

When we understand that one aspect of prayer is communion, we can fill in our hours and moments with quiet peace. Whenever I am compelled to wait for something—a plane, a train, an elevator—I have learned over the years to head off the possible frustration by forestalling it with communion prayer. Thus, the destructive is pushed out and the constructive comes in.

"A Moving Shrine"

This idea was given me by my old college principal, John Wallace, who once said to me: "Selwyn, where does your mind go whenever it has nowhere to go?" I had to confess that it went more often than not to thoughts of worry and concern. He suggested to me that whenever I found myself with nothing to focus on, I drop into my heart in prayer and use the moments to commune with God. What a change that suggestion made to my life! I offer it to you in the hope that it will do for you what it has done for me. What sweetness there is in the heart when one is able at a time of potential frustration to turn the conflict moment into a communion moment.

Oxenham puts it in these lines:

A little place of mystic grace
Of sin and self swept bare
Where I may look into Thy face
And talk with Thee in prayer.

Then the heart becomes what someone has called "a moving shrine" from which there arises the continual incense of adoration and love. When we can do this, then we are always at home in God—and thus never alone.

My Father and my God, drive the conviction deep within me that You are my home and thus I am never alone. Show me how to forestall the moments of possible conflict with moments of communion. This I ask in Jesus' peerless and precious Name. Amen.

TURN THE CONFLICT MOMENT INTO A
COMMUNION MOMENT.

I find that if
I seek God first,

it saves so

much time,

worry,

and uncertainty.

—Fiona Castle

Journal Entry

_____

_____

_____

_____

_____

_____

_____

_____

_____

_____

_____

_____

_____

_____

_____

_____

_____

_____

_____

_____

WEEK 4

HOW TO PRAY

God taught me

that he is as real when

I do not sense him

as when I do.

— Anne Townsend

A S C A F F O L D I N G
F O R P R A Y E R

"If you confess with your mouth, 'Jesus is Lord,' and
believe in your heart that God raised him from the dead,
you will be saved. For it is with your heart that you believe
and are justified, and it is with your mouth that you confess
and are saved. As the Scripture says, 'Anyone who trusts in
him will never be put to shame.' For there is no difference
between Jew and Gentile—the same Lord is Lord of all and
richly blesses all who call on him, for, 'Everyone who calls on
the name of the Lord will be saved.'"

Romans 10:9—13

Having seen, over the past three weeks, the meaning
and importance of prayer, we turn now to focus on the
steps we must take to establish an effective and powerful
prayer life. Over the years I have written extensively on the
subject of prayer; what I am about to say now represents my
latest thinking on the subject. Over these next twenty-eight
days I want to erect a scaffolding of suggestions which can
be taken down when the building is established. Some of
you will not need much help here as you already have a
healthy prayer life, but, even so, I hope that what I say will
be helpful, if only to reinforce the conviction that prayer is
one of life's most important spiritual exercises.

Before All Else

The first step is this—ensure that you know the Lord as your personal Savior before you attempt to establish a daily or regular prayer time with Him. Building a disciplined life of prayer is not the way to salvation. Jesus is the only Savior and the only means of salvation. This means that you cannot earn salvation by religious duties or regular devotional exercises. If you are not a child of His, then this moment turn your life over to Him by repenting of your sins and receiving from His hands the gift of eternal life.

When I was in my teens, a friend shared with me that he was unable to relate socially to girls of his own age because he didn't know what to say. One day he fell in love, and after that he couldn't stop talking. "True religion," someone said, "is falling in love with God." When you fall in love with God and His Son, the Lord Jesus Christ, then, believe me, prayer takes on a completely new dimension.

Father, help me to establish a greater prayer life
than I have ever known before. I know that
I shall stumble at times, but when I do, help me to
stumble in Your direction. When I fall, help me
to fall on my knees. In Jesus' Name. Amen.

WHEN YOU FALL IN LOVE WITH GOD AND HIS SON, PRAYER
TAKES ON A COMPLETELY NEW DIMENSION.

E A G E R   A N D

W I L L I N G

"So I say to you: Ask and it will be given to you; seek and you will find; knock and the door will be opened to you. For everyone who asks receives; he who seeks finds; and to him who knocks, the door will be opened. Which of you fathers, if your son asks for a fish, will give him a snake instead? Or if he asks for an egg, will give him a scorpion? If you, then, though you are evil, know how to give good gifts to your children, how much more will your Father in heaven give the Holy Spirit to those who ask him!"

Luke 11:9–13

Now that it is clear that building an effective prayer life is not the way to salvation but is a natural consequence of being saved, we are ready to focus on the next step—breathe a prayer for help as you begin. You are starting something which will make the difference between weakness and strength, defeat and victory, emptiness and fullness—so throw yourself upon the Lord at the outset.

Expect that you will come up against a few failures and difficulties as you attempt to establish an effective prayer life, and be patient with yourself as you bump up against problems. Always remember, however, that if there are any failures in prayer they are never failures on God's part; He never fails. Adopting this attitude at the start—that you need God's help and strength to do what He commands—will keep you alert to the fact that without Him you can do nothing.

Two-Way Communication

One of the greatest encouragements I received when I set out many years ago to establish a more effective prayer life was a short passage I read in a book. It went something like this: "God is far more interested and eager to establish a regular relationship with you in prayer than you could ever earn. You do not have to overcome His reluctance; you simply have to lay hold on His highest willingness." That was the catalyst I needed. The more I pondered the thought that God was actually willing and eager to enter into two-way communication with me through prayer, the more eager and willing I became to enter into it, too. Now, several decades later, I can testify that nothing is as wonderful as daily communication with God in prayer.

O God, I see that in relation to this matter of prayer, all Your barriers are down. Help me also to have no barriers. May my eagerness to communicate with You match Your eagerness to communicate with me. In Jesus' Name I ask it. Amen.

NOTHING IS AS WONDERFUL AS DAILY COMMUNICATION WITH GOD IN PRAYER.

THE POWER OF
FIFTEEN MINUTES

"Finally, all of you, live in harmony with one another; be sympathetic, love as brothers, be compassionate and humble. Do not repay evil with evil or insult with insult, but with blessing, because to this you were called so that you may inherit a blessing. For, 'Whoever would love life and see good days must keep his tongue from evil and his lips from deceitful speech. He must turn from evil and do good; he must seek peace and pursue it. For the eyes of the Lord are on the righteous and his ears are attentive to their prayer, but the face of the Lord is against those who do evil.'"

1 Peter 3:8–12

My next suggestion for establishing an effective prayer life is this—decide how much time you will give to the regular exercise of prayer. Note the word *decide*, for the matter must be an issue of the will and not be left to the ebb and flow of feeling. It is better to begin with a little amount of time and then increase it, than to start with a large block of time and find that you have taken on too great a task. Start with fifteen minutes—one can hardly get anywhere with less—and then week by week add to it if you can.

What God Can Do

Many years ago a woman wrote to me saying that she would like to establish a regular prayer time but at the moment she was far too busy. I encouraged her to begin by putting a fence around fifteen minutes of each day—and spend five minutes reading the Bible, five minutes meditating on what she had read, and five minutes talking to God in prayer. Two weeks later she wrote back excitedlyand said, 'Why, it's marvelous. After fifteen minutes a day with God I seem to get through my work in half the time. My mind is so clear that I can plan ahead in a way I was never able to do before. It's utterly incredible what God can do with fifteen minutes." I wrote back immediately and said, "If God can do that with fifteen minutes, just think what He could do with an hour!" She took the point and slowly increased her prayer time to one hour a day. I met that woman some years later in a Christian conference, and she told me that she could not get through a day with less than an hour and a half in prayer.

But I say again, when you begin, watch that you don't set your goals too high. Start with fifteen minutes a day and see where you go from there.

Gracious and loving Father, help me to establish the proper priorities in my life, and to put a prayer time with You high on my list. I know that if I don't choose my priorities, then life will choose them for me. in Jesus' Name I ask it. Amen.

PRAYER MUST BE AN ISSUE OF THE WILL AND NOT BE LEFT TO THE EBB AND FLOW OF FEELING.

DAY 4

PRAYING AGAINST DISINCLINATION

"I remember the days of long ago; I meditate on all your works and consider what your hands have done. I spread out my hands to you; my soul thirsts for you like a parched land. Answer me quickly, O LORD; my spirit fails. Do not hide your face from me or I will be like those who go down to the pit. Let the morning bring me word of your unfailing love, for I have put my trust in you. Show me the way I should go, for to you I lift up my soul. Rescue me from my enemies, O LORD, for I hide myself in you. Teach me to do your will, for you are my God; may your good Spirit lead me on level ground."

Psalm 143:5–10

The suggestion I want to put before you today is one that was given to me in my teens and is, in my opinion, one of the best pieces of advice I was ever given—keep your appointment with God whether you feel like it or not. I would be less than honest if I were to give you the impression that all your prayer times will be full of spiritual vitality and excitement. The most noble vocations have their times of drudgery, and prayer has them too. I have to confess that if my own times of prayer were conducted entirely on feeling alone, then they would be few and far between. We must learn to keep our appointment with God even when we don't feel like it. What would we think of someone who canceled an important appointment with us simply because he or she did not "feel like it"?

To say the least, we would view it as disrespectful and discourteous. Let's be sure that we treat God the way we ourselves would like to be treated.

Exercising Faith

It is a mistake to think that prayer is only effective when it arises from an eager and excited heart. Faith, not feeling, measures the efficacy of prayer. In fact, committing ourselves to praying when we don't feel like it greatly strengthens faith. Just as physical exercise builds up muscles in the body, so going to prayer when we don't feel inclined to do so builds up the muscles of faith. And, as you know, Jesus put great emphasis on faith. He never said to anyone, "Your feelings have made you whole," but on more than one occasion He said, "Your faith has made you whole."

Faith only develops as it is exercised. You rise higher on the scale of faith when you use the faith you have. So make an appointment with God—and keep it.

O God, help me pursue this task of prayer with firmness and resolution. Give me the will to pray so that commitment overwhelms every disinclination. This I ask in and through the peerless and precious Name of Jesus. Amen.

FAITH, NOT FEELING, MEASURES THE EFFICACY OF PRAYER.

THIRTY DAYS
MAKE A HABIT

"Devote yourselves to prayer, being watchful and thankful. And pray for us, too, that God may open a door for our message, so that we may proclaim the mystery of Christ, for which I am in chains. Pray that I may proclaim it clearly, as I should. Be wise in the way you act toward outsiders; make the most of every opportunity. Let your conversation be always full of grace, seasoned with salt, so that you may know how to answer everyone."

Colossians 4:2–6

Every serious Christian needs a pattern or plan for praying. It need not be complicated and it must not be imprisoning. But it should be plain and firm and observed with honest constancy—hence these suggestions that I am putting before you day by day.

Another suggestion for establishing an effective prayer life is this—organize your day around your prayer time and not your prayer time around your day. In other words, as far as is possible, fix the time when you are going to pray and let it stay fixed so that each day you do not have to debate the question. I say, "as far as possible," because there will be some days when, with the best will in the world, you will not be able to keep to your schedule. When that happens, don't despair but get back on track as soon as you can. Some may find it difficult to schedule a fixed time each day—difficult but not impossible. Growth in the matter of prayer demands iron firmness and, as the saying goes, where there's a will, there's a way.

The Ideal Habit

The advantage of a fixed time for prayer is this—the discipline quickly builds itself into one's life and takes on the solidarity of good habit. It soon has the regularity and naturalness of our mealtimes. Psychologists tell us that if we do something day after day for a period of thirty days, then it becomes part of our life and a habit is formed. What better habit can one form than the habit of prayer? Of course, we should not limit our praying to the prayers offered in those guarded and unhurried periods. We can pray anywhere—on the street, in the car, and so on—but let these unpremeditated prayers be extras, not substitutes.

O Father, forgive me that my life is regulated more by the things of time than the things of eternity. Give me the mind to pray, the love to pray, and the will to pray. In Jesus' Name I ask it. Amen.

GROWTH IN MATTER OF PRAYER DEMANDS IRON FIRMNESS.

THE MORNING
IS BEST

"The Sovereign LORD has given me an instructed tongue, to know the word that sustains the weary. He wakens me morning by morning, wakens my ear to listen like one being taught. The Sovereign LORD has opened my ears, and I have not been rebellious; I have not drawn back. I offered my back to those who beat me, my cheeks to those who pulled out my beard; I did not hide my face from mocking and spitting. Because the Sovereign LORD helps me, I will not be disgraced. Therefore have I set my face like flint, and I know I will not be put to shame."

Isaiah 50:4–7

We continue meditating on how to build an effective prayer life. My next suggestion is this—let your fixed time of prayer be as close to the beginning of the day as possible. There is a good reason for this—if you fix your prayer time at the end of the day, then it will be backward looking. If you fix it at the beginning of the day, it will be forward looking. In a previous meditation we saw how in the Garden of Gethsemane Jesus finished His prayer time with the words: "Rise, let us be going" (Matt. 26:46 NKJV). Prayer at the beginning of the day enables you to say, as Jesus said, "Rise, let us be going"—going to meet anything the day may bring.

Strength for the Day

The Psalms are filled with admonitions on praying to God at the beginning of the day: "In the morning my prayer comes before you" (Ps. 88:13). "I rise before dawn and cry for help; I have put my hope in your word" (119:147). "In the morning I will sing of your love" (59:16). Of course, if you can't take time in the morning, then take any time you can—but the morning is best. One Christian writer talks about the beginning of the day in these terms. "The pure strong hours of the morning when the soul of the day is at its best."

Wash your heart and mind in the presence of Christ before you go out to face the day. James Russell Lowell says:

Every morning lean thine arm awhile
Upon the window sill of heaven
And gaze upon thy God.
Then, with the vision in thy heart,
Turn strong to meet the day.

Father, help me not to step over the threshold of the day until I have taken time to turn to You for spiritual renewal and replenishment. Without You—not one step over the threshold; with You—anywhere. Amen.

WASH YOUR HEART AND MIND IN THE PRESENCE OF CHRIST BEFORE YOU GO OUT TO FACE THE DAY.

DEAF TO

DISTRACTION

"And when you pray, do not be like the hypocrites, for they love to pray standing in the synagogues and on the street corners to be seen by men. I tell you the truth, they have received their reward in full. But when you pray, go into your room, close the door and pray to your Father, who is unseen. Then your Father, who sees what is done in secret, will reward you. And when you pray, do not keep on babbling like pagans, for they think they will be heard because of their many words. Do not be like them, for your Father knows what you need before you ask him."

Matthew 6:5–8

My next suggestion for building an effective prayer life is this—choose carefully the place or environment in which you pray. Try to ensure that it is as favorable as possible—private, quiet, comfortable, and conducive to prayer. I conduct my personal prayer time in the room where I study, and, because I have prayed there so many times, the associations are such that I feel like dropping on my knees as soon as I open the door.

Of course, for some people, finding a private or quiet place in which to pray will be an impossibility—those who live in overcrowded homes or share a room with someone, for example. If you find yourself in this situation, then go to some place corresponding to the "closet" of which Jesus spoke—a place where you will be alone without disturbance. And if you can't do that, then learn to make your own "closet" by the power of inward withdrawal. Learn to "shut the door" even amid conditions that would otherwise bring disturbance.

The Sacred Chamber

A Christian lawyer I know, who commuted every working day from his home to the center of the city, told me that he used the forty-five-minute journey as an opportunity to pray. "How do you do it?" I asked. "I have learned to become deaf to distractions," he said. "As soon as the train pulls out of the station I climb the stairs to the sacred chamber of my imagination and I picture myself meeting with the Lord. Every morning He greets me with a smile and says: 'I'm glad you've come.'"

Admittedly, it took him some time to develop this art, but with perseverance anyone who finds it difficult to conduct prayer time in private can learn to build a chapel in the soul.

Father, help me remember that, though
there may be difficulties in finding a private
place to pray, as one hymn writer put it:
'Where'er we seek Thee, Thou art found, and
every place is hallowed ground.' Amen.

LEARN TO BUILD A CHAPEL IN THE SOUL.

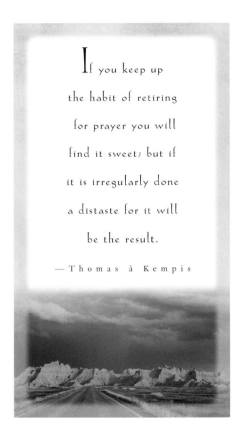

If you keep up
the habit of retiring
for prayer you will
find it sweet; but if
it is irregularly done
a distaste for it will
be the result.

—Thomas à Kempis

PRACTICING
PRAYER

Just before he died,
my younger brother, completely
disabled by Parkinson's disease
and cancer, said to me,
"Isn't it wonderful that, even
though I can do nothing else,
I can still pray?"

— Patricia St. John

"SETTLING DOWN IN GOD"

"We have a strong city; God makes salvation its walls and ramparts. Open the gates that the righteous nation may enter, the nation that keeps faith. You will keep in perfect peace him whose mind is steadfast, because he trusts in you. Trust in the LORD forever, for the LORD, the LORD, is the Rock eternal. He humbles those who dwell on high, he lays the lofty city low; he levels it to the ground and casts it down to the dust. Feet trample it down—the feet of the oppressed, the footsteps of the poor."

Isaiah 26:1b–6

Another suggestion that is helpful when preparing to pray is this—go into your prayer time relaxed and receptive. The Quakers used to call this "settling down in God." First, you should relax your body. Some might question this and say: "Prayer is a matter of the spirit—why waste time talking about the body?" However, the physical is often the gateway to the spiritual. If the physical is out of sorts, the spirit may find it difficult to soar. Take a few deep breaths (at least five) and let your body go loose. Picture a jellyfish, limp and floppy. In your mind's eye see yourself like that.

Rest Assured

But deeper than the body, the spirit must also be relaxed. No amount of physical relaxation techniques will work if the tension is in the spirit. Don't fall for the modern idea that to get a foothold in life all you need to do is learn how to relax physically. Unless you can trust the living God, surrender your affairs into His hands, and believe in His Word through thick and thin, you have no solid basis for victory. To relax spiritually, you must hold before you the fact that God is in control of everything and nothing can happen in your life that He and you can't handle together. Focus on that as you go to prayer and see if it doesn't help you "settle down in God."

"How did you like your flight?" asked a friend of a nervous passenger who had flown for the first time. "Very well," said the man, "but I didn't put my whole weight down during the entire trip." You cannot enjoy a flight, nor can you enjoy the journey through life, unless you learn to put your whole weight down. And there is nothing, absolutely nothing, upon which you can put your whole weight—except God.

Father, help me to enter every prayer session with "my whole weight down." Let me remind myself every time I bow my knees that by faith I am linked to You, the living God, and have the backing of an eternal purpose. In Jesus' Name I ask it. Amen.

GO INTO YOUR PRAYER TIME RELAXED AND RECEPTIVE.

H I S   T H O U G H T S —
Y O U R   T H O U G H T S

"For the word of God is living and active. Sharper than any double-edged sword, it penetrates even to dividing soul and spirit, joints and marrow; it judges the thoughts and attitudes of the heart. Nothing in all creation is hidden from God's sight. Everything is uncovered and laid bare before the eyes of him to whom we must give account."

Hebrews 4:12–13

Today I want to share with you a suggestion concerning prayer that the great George Müller of Bristol claimed was one of the greatest discoveries of his Christian experience—prime the pump of prayer by reading and meditating on the Scriptures. Let God speak to you through His Word before you speak to Him through your words.

The Presence of the Master

Reading and meditating on the Scriptures gives a climate to your prayer time and starts you thinking in the right direction. A few verses of Scripture reverently read will bring a Christian more speedily than anything else into the conscious presence of the Master. It will not be hard to converse with Christ when you already feel He is near.

This was the thought in my mind when I began writing *Every Day with Jesus* Bible reading notes. I said to myself, "If I can get Christians to spend a little time in the Word of God each day, then it will add fuel to their prayer lives." The fact that it has done so for thousands upon thousands of people is one of the great joys of my life.

A husband and wife once told me that they were getting very little out of their daily quiet times. "Tell me how you begin," I said. "We just sit and think about anything that comes to mind," they answered. "Thank you," I replied, "you have just told me your problem. You are defeated in prayer because you depend on your own thoughts to prime the pump rather than on God's thoughts." They listened to my advice, began their prayer times with the reading of Scripture, and went on to experience a powerful new life of prayer. Begin with your own thoughts and you become self-engrossed; begin with His—and His thoughts will become your thoughts.

Father, I am so thankful that You have given me this wonderful book, the Bible, which, when I look into it, unfolds for me Your mind and purposes for my life. Help me not only to love it but to live in it. In Jesus' Name. Amen.

IT WILL NOT BE HARD TO CONVERSE WITH CHRIST WHEN YOU ALREADY FEEL HE IS NEAR.

THE BOOK THAT READS YOU

"'For my thoughts are not your thoughts, neither are your ways my ways,' declares the LORD. 'As the heavens are higher than the earth, so are my ways higher than your ways and my thoughts than your thoughts. As the rain and snow come down from heaven, and do not return to it without watering the earth and making it bud and flourish, so that it yields seed for the sower and bread for the eater, so is my word that goes out from my mouth: It will not return to me empty, but will accomplish what I desire and achieve the purpose for which I sent it.'"

Isaiah 55:8–11

Many people who read the Bible do not derive from it the benefit they ought because they fail to come to it with the right attitude of mind. Hence a further suggestion to add to what I said yesterday—do not be content just to read the Bible, but be willing to let the Bible read you. A mistake made by many Christians in their approach to the Bible is to come to it looking more for confirmation or encouragement than for challenge and correction. But the Bible is more convicting than comforting, more challenging than confirming.

Evil Exposed

I am not saying that the Bible does not speak to us when we need encouragement, because quite clearly it does. What I am saying is this—traumas and emotional upheavals apart, the major impact of Scripture on us ought to be its exposure of our self-centeredness, our wrong thinking, and our spiritual waywardness. Jim Packer, the well-known theologian, puts it like this: "The impact of Scripture is more shocking than supportive. When I come to the Scripture, I assume I am wrong. What else can you expect? My perspectives clash violently with the Bible." Lawrence Crabb puts the same point in these words: "We will not understand the Bible aright until we come to it willing to be exposed by it."

Because our thoughts are so contrary to God's thoughts, we ought to be ready and willing to let the Bible read us whenever we open its pages. The fear of being read by this book means that many people fail to get the best out of it. May I suggest that if you are having a comfortable time reading the Bible, the chances are you are not reading it correctly.

O Father, I see so clearly that my attitude
toward Your Word determines what I will get
out of it. Help me to approach it not simply as
a book to be read, but as a book that reads me.
In Jesus' Name I pray. Amen.

THE BIBLE IS MORE CONVICTING THAN COMFORTING, MORE
CHALLENGING THAN CONFIRMING.

THE DEVINE CATHARSIS

"This is the message we have heard from him and declare to you: God is light; in him there is no darkness at all. If we claim to have fellowship with him yet walk in the darkness, we lie and do not live by the truth. But if we walk in the light, as he is in the light, we have fellowship with one another, and the blood of Jesus, his Son, purifies us from all sin. If we claim to be without sin, we deceive ourselves and the truth is not in us. If we confess our sins, he is faithful and just and will forgive us our sins and purify us from all unrighteousness. If we claim we have not sinned, we make him out to be a liar and his word has no place in our lives."

1 John 1:5–10

Once you have spent time reading and meditating on the Scriptures—what next? Deal at once with anything God may have brought to your notice during your time of meditation. Spiritual maturity is defined by our willingness and eagerness to set about correcting any known spiritual violation, and doing it as quickly as possible after it has been made known. The discipline of gazing into the mirror of God's Word, the Bible, when undertaken with seriousness and a willingness to have one's life read by the greatest of all authorities, will have inevitable consequences. Even to the smug, the searchlight of the Word reveals the selfishness and pride that is deeply embedded in human nature. It was to the surface our deeply held resentments, self-centered motivations, hidden jealousies, and the latent lust as well.

The Prayer of Confession

How does one deal with these revealed problems? Does one press on and pray about other things, leaving the confession of them until later? No, it's best to deal with them right away, before going any further into your devotions. Confess the spiritual violation to God and ask for His forgiveness. Commit yourself, also, to drawing upon His grace so that in the future any repetition of the problem may be avoided.

When this is done, then reach out for the forgiveness that so freely follows on the heels of the prayer of confession. It will flow over you like a river. The Greeks had a word for what I am describing now—it is called "catharsis." It means a radical cleansing, the discharge of all impurities, the draining of all defilement. After this divine catharsis, one goes into the prayer time feeling clean and new on the inside.

O Jesus, Your blood continually avails for me so I can be immersed in that cleansing fountain and find myself with a purity that is not my own. Help me be as ready to draw nigh to You as You are to me. For Your own dear Name's sake. Amen.

SPIRITUAL MATURITY IS DEFINED BY OUR WILLINGNESS TO SEE ABOUT CORRECTING ANY KNOWN SPIRITUAL VIOLATION.

BEING EXTRAVAGANT WITH PRAISE

"Shout for joy to the LORD, all the earth. Worship the LORD with gladness; come before him with joyful songs. Know that the LORD is God. It is he who made us, and we are his; we are his people, the sheep of his pasture. Enter his gates with thanksgiving and his courts with praise; give thanks to him and praise his name. For the LORD is good and his love endures forever; his faithfulness continues through all generations."

Psalm 100:1–5

We continue from where we left off yesterday. Assuming one is standing in the presence of God with no consciousness of unconfessed sin, what does one need to do to begin a time of prayer? My suggestion is this—let your first focus be adoration, thanksgiving, and praise.

Heartfelt Thanksgiving

Adore God in your heart. Ponder the fact that you, a soiled sinner, are allowed to enter into the presence of God and to linger there as long as you like. Remind yourself again of the thrilling truth that the world is not the sporting ground of half-mad men but that God has everything in His hands. Human freedom is real, but it is limited. It might look at times as though the world is out of control, but this is only the appearance of things. We live in a guarded universe, and God will have the last word. Remember, no matter how sensational the world's headlines, no atomic device can ever blast the pillars of the cosmos. So adore God, praise Him, rejoice in Him, and thank Him for His everlasting love. Be extravagant with your praise. Let it not be given to Him in thimblefuls; do as Mary did in the Gospels and break open the alabaster box of your soul.

If you have difficulty here, let your mind run over the many reasons you have to be thankful: health, home, love, friends, creation's beauty, work, service, prayer . . . and so on. If honesty compels you to admit that you do not enjoy some of the things I have listed, then think of the God-given things you do enjoy. Think on them—think on them until your heart swells with gratitude and thanksgiving rises like a tidal wave within your soul.

O Father, forgive me that I am so sparing with my praise when I have so much to be thankful for. Help me have a clear focus on how good You are to me, and cause me always to come into Your courts with thanksgiving. In Jesus' Name I ask it. Amen.

THINK ON THE GOD-GIVEN THINGS YOU ENJOY UNTIL
YOUR HEART SWELLS WITH GRATITUDE.

THREE AVENUES
TO THE THRONE!

"It is good to praise the LORD and make music to your name, O Most High, to proclaim your love in the morning and your faithfulness at night, to the music of the ten-stringed lyre and the melody of the harp. For you make me glad by your deeds, O LORD; I sing for joy at the works of your hands. How great are your works, O LORD, how profound your thoughts!"

Psalm 92:1–5

So many Christians appear not to understand the difference between adoration, thanksgiving, and praise that I feel a day defining the difference between these three words might be helpful. Adoration is the creaturely bending of the knee or the bowing of the heart before the Creator, the upward look of the soul to the face of Him who is all and in all. It transcends language and goes far beyond the province of asking anything—either for oneself or others. It is unconcerned about needs, and it desires only to stand in the dazzling presence of Him who is eternal light. For this reason *adoration* and *worship* are similar terms.

God's Many Blessings

Thanksgiving is different. We adore and worship God for who He is, but we thank Him for what He does. It is simply saying "thank You" to the One who bestows so much blessing on our lives. A Christian man once told me he could never engage in thanksgiving because he had nothing to be thankful for. Nothing to be thankful for! God forgive the thought. No appreciation of the mercy that chastens us in our pride and pleasure, or of the problems that drive us to distraction yet at the same time push us, humbled, penitent, and receptive, into the arms of an omnipotent God? We have only to focus our minds on God's blessings, and endless cause for thanksgiving passes by in review.

Praise is different still. Praise means "to speak well of, to exalt, to honor" and implies the use of words and language. It is usually enthusiastic and joyful and can be accompanied with music, singing, and even dancing.

Adoration, thanksgiving, and praise—three avenues to the eternal throne.

O Father, help me to make use of these three avenues to glory that are available to me whenever I approach Your eternal throne. Forgive me that so often I am more concerned with getting than with giving. In Jesus' Name I pray. Amen.

ADORATION, THANKSGIVING, AND PRAISE—
THREE AVENUES TO THE ETERNAL THRONE.

THE KING OF KING'S COUNSEL

"In the same way, the Spirit helps us in our weakness. We do not know what we ought to pray for, but the Spirit himself intercedes for us with groans that words cannot express. And he who searches our hearts knows the mind of the Spirit, because the Spirit intercedes for the saints in accordance with God's will. And we know that in all things God works for the good of those who love him, who have been called according to his purpose. For those God foreknew he also predestined to be conformed to the likeness of his Son, that he might be the firstborn among many brothers. And those he predestined, he also called; those he called, he also justified; those he justified, he also glorified."

Romans 8:26–30

My next-to-last suggestion in relation to the matter of building a more effective prayer life is this—open your whole being to the flow of God's Spirit. Sometimes one hears the expression: "I need all the help I can get." Ever said that? Well, if Christians are to exercise their rights and privileges at the place of prayer, to achieve great victories, and to reach new spiritual heights, then they need all the spiritual help they can get. We have all the help we need in the person of the Holy Spirit. Who is the Holy Spirit? He is the third person of the Trinity, and one of His executive functions is to minister the resources of God and Christ to the weak and helpless.

When Prayer Is Difficult

The law will not allow any person to stand accused in a court of law without a professional advocate to plead his or her case. If the accused is unable to provide the advocate, then the state assumes the responsibility. God does something similar for those who sometimes find it difficult to pray—He provides us not with a legal counsel but with the King of king's Counsel—the blessed Holy Spirit. As our text for today states, He comes alongside and lights in us the passion and flame of prayer.

There will be times, too, when you experience what is called the gift of infused prayer, when the Holy Spirit does more than help you to pray but actually prays in you. This will not happen every day, but the more you pray, the more you open yourself to the possibility. Believe me, no greater awe can grip the human soul than the awe that comes when you sense you are not just praying but being prayed through.

Gracious and loving Father, how thankful I am that You have given me a divine Advocate who comes alongside to help me pray. I am thankful, too, for those moments of infused prayer when I am not only helped to pray but prayed through. Amen.

THE HOLY SPIRIT COMES ALONGSIDE AND LIGHTS IN US THE PASSION AND FLAME OF PRAYER.

There is a way of ordering our mental life on more than one level at once. On one level we may be thinking, discussing, seeing, calculating, meeting all the demands of external affairs. But deep within, behind the scenes, at a profounder level, we may also be in prayer and adoration, song and worship, and a gentle receptiveness to divine breathings.

—Thomas Kelly

Journal Entry

PRAYERS OF PETITION

When thou prayest,

rather let thy heart

be without words

than thy words

without heart.

— John Bunyan

FATHER!

"How great is the love the Father has lavished on us, that we should be called children of God! And that is what we are! The reason the world does not know us is that it did not know him. Dear friends, now we are children of God, and what we will be has not yet been made known. But we know that when he appears, we shall be like him, for we shall see him as he is. Everyone who has this hope in him purifies himself, just as he is pure."

1 John 3:1–3

Once you have primed the pump of your soul by reading and meditating on the Scriptures, made any confession that is necessary, focused on how good God is and given Him your adoration, thanksgiving, and praise—what next? This—make your requests known to God in an attitude of humility and childlike faith. I say "childlike" faith because when we pray we are children coming before our heavenly Father. Never forget that God is a Father—with a father's heart and a father's love.

Childlike Faith

When Jesus taught the disciples to pray in the form we know as the Lord's Prayer, He told them to begin with the fact that God is our heavenly Father. This is important because we can never rise higher in our understanding of prayer than our concept of God. If we see God as someone other than Father, then we will be fearful to approach Him. We will wonder whether He has our best interests at heart, and the wondering will lead to a sabotaging of our prayers. How can you come confidently before God in prayer and ask of Him the things you need if deep down in your heart you do not see Him as a warm, compassionate, loving, heavenly Father? Any doubts about His willingness and eagerness to give will short-circuit your petitions, and, though you ask, it will not be with childlike faith.

A child who has no doubts about his father's warmth and love does not beat about the bush. He comes confidently into his father's presence and asks for what he wants, knowing that, though his petition may not be granted, he himself will be received with warmth, affection, and love. So must we.

O God, how tenderly wise You are in that You put first things first. You have shown me that the petitions I ask of You must be preceded by correct thoughts of You. You are my Father—and I am Your child. Let this relationship permeate all my praying. Amen.

WE CAN NEVER RISE HIGHER IN OUR UNDERSTANDING OF PRAYER THAN OUR CONCEPT OF GOD.

A C U R B T O
I N D E P E N D E N C E

"Take heed, you senseless ones among the people; you fools, when will you become wise? Does he who implanted the ear not hear? Does he who formed the eye not see? Does he who disciplines nations not punish? Does he who teaches man lack knowledge? The LORD knows the thoughts of man; he knows that they are futile."

Psalm 94:8–11

My next suggestion is this—talk to God continually about the things you need (the usual term for this is *petition*). Don't be afraid to ask God for things. Our Lord encouraged petition—and persistent petition too. Had He not done so, we might have hesitated to include personal petition in our prayers on the grounds that God knows what we need and can be trusted to give it to us.

The Source of Life

Why did our Lord put a high priority on petition? There are, of course, many reasons, but let me pick out the one that I feel is primary—He encouraged petition in order that we might have a clear understanding of our deep dependency on Him. The biggest struggle we have in the Christian life is with the legacy that we received from Adam—a spirit of independence. In the Garden of Eden sin was a declaration of independence in which Adam and Eve established their own system of living over against God's. At first they looked up into the face of God in adoration, thanksgiving and praise, and worshiped Him as dependent beings; they talked with Him and He with them. But the moment came when they preferred independence to dependence.

The attitude of independence is with us still; it is tightly wedged in our fallen human nature. Prayer, especially petitionary prayer which causes us to bow the knee before God and ask Him for things, curbs that independent spirit and helps us acknowledge that He is the source of our life. God encourages our dependency on Him not because He delights to be boss, but because we were made to be dependent beings and we function best when we live in dependency on Him.

O Father, how can I sufficiently thank You that You will not have me dumb in the hour of my need but You encourage me to ask You for things. And Your ear is ever open to Your children's needy cry. Thank You, dear Father. Thank You. Amen.

PETITION GIVES US A CLEAR UNDERSTANDING OF OUR DEEP DEPENDENCY ON GOD.

PRAYING IN JESUS' NAME

"Jesus answered . . . 'How can you say, "Show us
the Father"? Don't you believe that I am in the Father, and
that the Father is in me? The words I say to you are not just
my own. Rather it is the Father, living in me, who is doing
his work. Believe me when I say that I am in the Father and
the Father is in me; or at least believe on the evidence of
the miracles themselves. I tell you the truth, anyone who
has faith in me will do what I have been doing. He will do
even greater things than these, because I am going to the
Father. And I will do whatever you ask in my name, so that
the Son may bring glory to the Father. You may ask me
or anything in my name, and I will do it.'"

John 14:9–14

Even though over the past days I have been referring
to the points I am making on building an effective prayer
life as "suggestions," you will, I am sure, realize that some
of the things I am calling "suggestions" are actually divine
commands. Today's "suggestion" is in that category—present
your petitions to God in and through the peerless
and precious Name of Jesus. Our text for today makes this
point perfectly clear—we are to offer our petitions to
God in Jesus' Name.

Christlike Prayer

But what does it mean to pray in Christ's Name?
Well, it means more than just attaching His Name to the end

of our prayers, for quite clearly His Name could be joined on to prayers that are crudely and utterly selfish. Praying in the Name of Jesus means praying according to the character of Christ, or praying prayers that He would pray if He were in our shoes. God can only answer prayer if it is in accord with the spirit of Jesus Christ. No matter how hard you pray "in the Name of Jesus," you will never get God to do anything that is not Christlike. And it is not just that He won't do it—He can't do it. It is impossible for God to do anything against His own nature. We must understand that when we pray in the Name of Jesus we are really asking that we might be caught up in the Spirit of Christ—whose sole aim, you remember, was to do the will of the Father—and put God's will as the highest priority in our lives.

So, the next time you ask God for something, say to yourself: Is this prayer in harmony with the Spirit of the Lord Jesus Christ? Is it consistent with His character? If so, then go ahead and use His Name. All heaven will stand behind it.

O Father, help me understand what it means
to pray in Jesus' Name. Save me from using
His Name as a kind of magical formula, but help
me soak my spirit in Christ's character so that
my prayer and my will coincide with His.
Truly I ask—in Jesus' Name. Amen.

GOD CAN ANSWER PRAYER ONLY IF IT IS IN ACCORD WITH
THE SPIRIT OF JESUS CHRIST.

G O D   H E A R S   Y O U

"Consider it pure joy, my brothers, whenever you face trials of many kinds, because you know that the testing of your faith develops perseverance. Perseverance must finish its work so that you may be mature and complete, not lacking anything. If any of you lacks wisdom, he should ask God, who gives generously to all without finding fault, and it will be given to him. But when he asks, he must believe and not doubt, because he who doubts is like a wave of the sea, blown and tossed by the wind. That man should not think he will receive anything from the Lord; he is a double-minded man, unstable in all he does."

James 1:2–8

We continue meditating on petitionary prayer and my next suggestion is this—always remember that God listens not just to your words but to you. I would stress the word *you*, not a part of you, a vagrant portion of you slipping into the prayer experience on the side, but the real you, the whole you, the full you.

Divided Personalities

What I am saying is this: so often the prayer of our lips does not match the prayer that we are praying deep down in our hearts. That is why so many of our prayers go unanswered. Our hearts are not at one with our lips; we are divided personalities. One of the strangest things I have come across in the years I have been counseling is the discovery that people express something with their lips while deep down in their hearts there are cross purposes. They like to hear themselves using the right words and the right phrases—it all sounds so good and spiritual—but what they say and what they ask for is not confirmed in the depths of their being.

A man I once counseled told me that he had prayed for something for years—something that was clearly in the will of God—but had never received it. As we talked, it became clear in the light of the Holy Spirit's illumination that there was a hidden fear in his heart that if God gave him what he asked for he would not be able to handle it. The hidden inner fear short-circuited his prayer; it made him a divided person. The reason he didn't get what he asked for was not because God was not willing to give, but because he was not willing to receive. God hears you—not merely what you say.

Father, I see that often I ask for something with my lips that does not have the backing of my heart. Then prayer becomes an illusion rather than an illumination. Help me, dear Father. I want to be a whole person. In Jesus' Name. Amen.

GOD HEARS *YOU*—NOT MERELY WHAT YOU SAY.

"P U T   I T   I N   W R I T I N G"

"Rejoice in the Lord always. I will say it again: Rejoice! Let your gentleness be evident to all. The Lord is near. Do not be anxious about anything, but in everything, by prayer and petition, with thanksgiving, present your requests to God. And the peace of God, which transcends all understanding, will guard your hearts and minds in Christ Jesus. Finally, brothers, whatever is true, whatever is noble, whatever is right, whatever is pure, whatever is lovely, whatever is admirable—if anything is excellent or praiseworthy—think about such things. Whatever you have learned or received or heard from me, or seen in me—put it into practice. And the God of peace will be with you."

Philippians 4:4—9

Here is another suggestion that might help you in relation to petitionary prayer—put your requests in writing. I do not mean by this that you have to write a formal letter to God, but that you identify your request in a written sentence or two. This is not for God's benefit, but for yours. Expression always deepens impression. I find that sometimes when I write something down I begin to see how unclear the thing really was to me. There are times, too, when, having written something down, I say to myself: My request has to be changed because it is not what I really want.

Clarity and Commitment

Writing a request down, then, has several advantages. First, it helps you decide what you really want and helps overcome the point we considered yesterday—a division of the personality. If the whole "you" does not really want the thing you are asking for, then your prayer will be blocked. Second, it means that if you are willing to commit yourself to something you have written on paper, you are probably serious about it and will stand behind it. Third (and this is a reinforcement of what I said above), the writing down of a request on paper inscribes it more deeply on your heart. The expression deepens the impression. Fourth, you commit yourself more fully to a line of action. Like Pilate (but for a different reason), you say, "What I have written, I have written" (John 19:22).

Writing a request down helps you consider whether you can back up your request with all your being. You must package your own request, or the answer will not be backed by God.

O Father, there is so much to learn about prayer—but I am a receptive student. Help me to commit myself to what I am asking for, and if writing down my requests assists in achieving this, then I will do it. In Jesus' Name. Amen.

EXPRESSION ALWAYS DEEPENS IMPRESSION.

GIVE ME, GIVE ME, GIVE ME....

"And why do you worry about clothes? See how the lilies of the field grow. They do not labor or spin. Yet I tell you that not even Solomon in all his splendor was dressed like one of these. If that is how God clothes the grass of the field, which is here today and tomorrow is thrown into the fire, will he not much more clothe you, O you of little faith? So do not worry, saying, 'What shall we eat?' or 'What shall we drink?' or 'What shall we wear?' For the pagans run after all these things, and your heavenly Father knows that you need them. But seek first his kingdom and his righteousness, and all these things will be given to you as well. Therefore do not worry about tomorrow, for tomorrow will worry about itself. Each day has enough trouble of its own."

Matthew 6:28–34

The great recurrent danger we must look out for when seeking to establish an effective prayer life is that of making our prayer all personal petition. "Give me . . . Give me . . . Give me . . ." We must guard against that just as vigilantly as we guard against the danger of having no prayer life at all. So here is my suggestion for today—keep petition in its proper perspective. As we have seen, petition has a legitimate place in the life of prayer, but don't let your prayer time be overloaded by it.

Seeking More of God

An interesting thing happens as we grow and mature in the life of prayer—we find we are asking less and less for things and seeking more and more of God. In the early part of my Christian life, petition took up most of my prayer time. I used to ask God for one thing after another—sometimes as many as twenty or thirty things in one session. Now things occupy only a minor part of my prayer life, and there are some days when I ask nothing for myself at all. This is because the text that is before us today has made a deepening impact on me over the years. I have come to realize that the more I seek God for Himself, and not for what He can do for me, the more He sees to it that I get the things I need. This does not mean that there will never be a need in my life to ask God for things, but it does mean that petitionary prayers that focus on my personal needs are not as important as they once were.

Am I growing? I would like to think so, but I didn't get there in one leap, and neither will you. Prayer is like a school in which we graduate from one level to another. And don't expect to jump a class.

Father, I see that I have to graduate in the school of prayer. Help me to be a good student and to be willing to develop at Your pace, not mine. I want to be as mature in prayer as it is possible to be. Teach me, my Father. In Jesus' Name. Amen.

PRAYER IS LIKE A SCHOOL IN WHICH WE GRADUATE FROM ONE LEVEL TO ANOTHER.

"HIS MASTER'S VOICE"

"Then came the Feast of Dedication at Jerusalem. It was winter, and Jesus was in the temple area walking in Solomon's Colonnade. The Jews gathered around him, saying, 'How long will you keep us in suspense? If you are the Christ, tell us plainly.' Jesus answered, 'I did tell you, but you do not believe. The miracles I do in my Father's name speak for me, but you do not believe because you are not my sheep. My sheep listen to my voice; I know them, and they follow me. I give them eternal life, and they shall never perish; no one can snatch them out of my hand. My Father, who has given them to me, is greater than all; no one can snatch them out of my Father's hand. I and the Father are one.' "

John 10:22–30

No discussion on the subject of prayer would be complete without reference to the need not only to talk with God but to let God talk to you. So here is my final suggestion—after you have talked to God, spend a little time letting God talk to you. The listening side of prayer is not easy; it has to be cultivated. At first a beginner is not able to disentangle God's voice from the voices that originate from inside him—the ghostly whisperings of the subconscious, the obsessive thoughts that clamor for attention, and so on.

Expectancy

The first essential is expectancy. When people say to me,

"I pray, but I never hear the voice of God," I ask, "But do you expect Him to speak to you?" The answer is usually, "No." Then I say, "Well, then, why are you disappointed?" Let me encourage you to take a notebook into your prayer time to put down anything God may say to you. A notebook is a sign of faith. It says, "I am expecting something to happen." Hundreds of people told me that this suggestion—taking a notebook into one's prayer time as a sign of faith—has done more than anything to transform their prayer time.

Does God speak every time we pray? Not usually, but, generally speaking, the more one waits, the more certain one will be of hearing His voice. What does His voice sound like? It is quiet, firm, and authoritative. Sometimes God will speak just a word like "Be not afraid;" at other times, a whole sentence. When you learn to recognize the Master's voice, you will be richly rewarded, for you will find that as He speaks your soul will quicken within you.

So go into your next prayer time expecting God to speak to you. Incline your ear, and in time you will not be disappointed.

Father, forgive me if I have neglected the listening side of prayer. Too often I say, "Lord, Your servant speaks," when I ought to be saying, "Speak, Lord, Your servant hears." Give me the right perspective. In Jesus' Name. Amen.

LET GOD TALK TO YOU.

A man prayed,
and at first he thought
that prayer was talking.
But he became more
and more quiet until
in the end he realized
that prayer is listening.

—Søren Kierkegaard

Journal Entry

WEEK 7

PRAYERS OF INTERCESSION

Meditation is the necessary

prelude to intercession.

We must hear, know . . .

and obey the will of God

before we pray it

into the lives of others.

— Richard Foster

THE CROWNING MINISTRY

"Abraham remained standing before the LORD. Then Abraham approached him and said: 'Will you sweep away the righteous with the wicked? What if there are fifty righteous people in the city? Will you really sweep it away and not spare the place for the sake of the fifty righteous people in it? Far be it from you to do such a thing—to kill the righteous with the wicked, treating the righteous and the wicked alike. Far be it from you! Will not the Judge of all the earth do right?' The LORD said, 'If I find fifty righteous people in the city of Sodom, I will spare the whole place for their sake.'"

Genesis 18:22b–26

We said yesterday that we must guard against the danger of spending too much time asking God for things for ourselves. This brings me to my suggestion for today—turn at some point in your prayer time to focus on the needs of others. It is impossible to develop a healthy prayer life without giving some attention to the needs of others. Apart from the fact that this prevents us from falling into the pit of selfishness, it enables us to cooperate with God in bringing about spiritual change in the lives of those who are in need. The action of focusing our prayers on the needs of others is called intercession. Someone has described this ministry as "the crowning ministry of the Christian life."

Concern for Others

But how do you intercede for others? First, see the person for whom you are praying, and his or her need, clearly in your mind. If you have never met and cannot visualize his or her appearance, focus just on the need. Then think about the power of God and His readiness to bless, and in the crucible of your loving heart, draw the person you are praying for close to God. Hold him or her there for as long as you feel it necessary. Like the friends of the paralytic in Mark 2:1–12, you are bringing that person to the feet of Jesus. Small as your love is beside God's, it is the channel that God has chosen to work through.

Believe that God is at work, touching that person in response to your loving and prayerful concern. If the person you are praying for is open to God, then infinite love and power will go to work and bring the divine purposes to pass. Your important ministry has been to make the link.

My Father and my God, I sense that the ministry
of intercession will cost me something in terms
of time, energy, and concern. You have given
much to me—help me now to give much to others.
I ask this in and through Your peerless
and precious Name. Amen.

IT IS IMPOSSIBLE TO DEVELOP A HEALTHY PRAYER LIFE
WITHOUT ATTENTION TO THE NEEDS OF OTHERS.

K E E P A L I S T

"The LORD looked and was displeased that there was no justice. He saw that there was no one, he was appalled that there was no one to intervene; so his own arm worked salvation for him, and his own righteousness sustained him. He put on righteousness as his breastplate, and the helmet of salvation on his head; he put on the garments of vengeance and wrapped himself in zeal as in a cloak. According to what they have done, so will he repay wrath to his enemies and retribution to his foes; he will repay the islands their due. From the west, men will fear the name of the LORD, and from the rising of the sun, they will revere his glory. For he will come like a pent-up flood that the breath of the Lord drives along."

Isaiah 59:15b—19

In talking about intercession, it must be understood that I am outlining here the requirements of an individual and not a corporate ministry of intercession. A corporate or group ministry is another subject and does not come within the scope of these present meditations. How does one go about developing an individual ministry of intercession? With method, of course. This, then, is my suggestion for today—keep a list of those people and causes for which you feel a special concern. To blunder into God's presence and chat about the people or things that happen to cross your mind is not the best way. There will be times, of course, when people's names will come to you in the middle of your prayer time, but that will be more the exception than the rule.

Be Selective

You need a prayer list. Names and causes should not be added lightly to it. Avoid the temptation to list all the things you *could* pray about, but list only the things you *should* pray about. The compilation and use of prayer lists are important tasks in themselves. Some people keep a short list that they use every day, an urgent list that is used perhaps for one or two days, and a general list that is used only occasionally.

Be sure of this—God will not want you to pray about all the people and all the causes that come into your mind. If you were to do that, you would finish up needing prayer yourself. Be selective. Whenever a person or issue comes into your mind or is brought to your attention, ask God: "Is this for me?" Watch for the witness of the Spirit that says, "Yes." Then trust God to lay the needs you feel no witness about on the hearts of others.

Loving Father, help me to have a spirit that is so sensitised to Your Spirit that I clearly hear Your voice and follow Your directions in all my intercessions. In Christ's Name I pray. Amen.

LIST ONLY THE THINGS YOU SHOULD PRAY ABOUT.

SPIRITUAL

BREATHLESSNESS

"I urge, then, first of all, that requests, prayers, intercession and thanksgiving be made for everyone—for kings and all those in authority, that we may live peaceful and quiet lives in all godliness and holiness. This is good, and pleases God our Savior, who wants all men to be saved and to come to a knowledge of the truth. For there is one God and one mediator between God and men, the man Christ Jesus, who gave himself as a ransom for all men—the testimony given in its proper time. And for this purpose I was appointed a herald and an apostle—I am telling the truth, I am not lying—and a teacher of the true faith to the Gentiles."

1 Timothy 2:1–7

An important suggestion or principle to remember in relation to intercession is this—intercession should always be unhurried.

Spiritual breathlessness and intercessory prayer do not go together. If, in the honest busyness of life, you can only give a limited time to intercession, then you ought to come to it as though you had all the time in the world. It must be noted, however, that we are often far busier than we ought to be, and a little thought and reevaluation of our schedules can often give us extra minutes—even hours.

Appropriating Time

I have known some Christians who have been so caught up in the ministry of intercession that they have cut down on things like sleep, socializing, watching television, listening to music, attending the movies, and so on, in order to give themselves to this highly important task. Some retired people give hours to it every day and make it the main ministry of their lives.

I have already pointed out what might be described as the dynamics of intercession—linking God and a person in need—and you will see from this definition that the quality of praying I am talking about here cannot be skimped. Running your eye quickly down a prayer list and saying, "Lord, bless so and so," will seem almost meaningless to those who understand what intercession is about. Indeed, it is right to say that intercession is such a demanding ministry that few feel they can undertake it in any significant way. However, every Christian should do what he or she can in this matter. Any time given to prayer for others will have its rewards. Nothing is too small, and nothing is too large.

O Father, I see the importance of intercession, but I am also aware of its cost. There is a fear in me that I am not able to rise to all that is required. But I do want to be involved—even if it is in a small way. Help me. In Jesus' Name. Amen.

ANY TIME GIVEN TO PRAYER FOR OTHERS
WILL HAVE ITS REWARDS.

WHEN NOTHING HAPPENS

"'Do not be afraid,' Samuel replied. 'You have done all this evil; yet do not turn away from the LORD, but serve the LORD with all your heart. Do not turn away after useless idols. They can do you no good, nor can they rescue you, because they are useless. For the sake of his great name the LORD will not reject his people, because the LORD was pleased to make you his own. As for me, far be it from me that I should sin against the LORD by failing to pray for you. And I will teach you the way that is good and right. But be sure to fear the LORD and serve him faithfully with all your heart; consider what great things he has done for you. Yet if you persist in doing evil, both you and your king will be swept away.'"

1 Samuel 12:20–25

We continue meditating on the theme of intercession. If God sent an angel to visit a powerhouse in one of our towns or cities today, where do you think he would go? It would be to the homes and churches where the intercessors are gathered. No one can even dream of the power that is generated through intercessory prayer. It can make more impact in the universe than any hydrogen bomb. Hence another suggestion concerning intercession—as long as you are sure that your prayer is in harmony with God's purposes, never give up. Sometimes, when you enter into intercession, weeks or months will go by with nothing appearing to happen, but as long as you sense God wants you to continue, keep on. Human nature is prone to weakness, and when we don't see results after we have prayed for a while, the temptation is to turn to other things. This is one of the disciplines of this important ministry—the discipline to keep going when there are no obvious results.

The Sacrifice of Time

But how do you know that God wants you to keep interceding? If your heart is open and sensitive to God—and this comes only as a result of much exposure to Him—you will feel a gentle pressure within you to persist. Follow that pressure, even though it costs the continued sacrifice of time. "Far be it from me," said Samuel to the stubborn Israelites, "that I should sin against the Lord by ending my prayers for you" (1 Sam. 12:23 TLB).

Human nature is stubborn stuff—your own is—but if you leave off praying, you close a channel to the stream of God's power. It is a solemn thought that we can sin against God by ceasing to pray for people whom He has laid on our hearts.

Father, give me the sensitivity of spirit to know how to pray, when to pray, and when not to stop praying. My own heart might say, "Enough," when Your heart says, "Go on." Grant always that Your voice may come through loud and clear. Amen.

WE CAN SIN AGAINST GOD BY CEASING TO PRAY.

PRAYER IS DYNAMITE!

"Is any one of you in trouble? He should pray. Is anyone happy? Let him sing songs of praise. Is any one of you sick? He should call the elders of the church to pray over him and anoint him with oil in the name of the Lord. And the prayer offered in faith will make the sick person well; the Lord will raise him up. If he has sinned, he will be forgiven. Therefore confess your sins to each other and pray for each other so that you may be healed. The prayer of a righteous man is powerful and effective. Elijah was a man just like us. He prayed earnestly that it would not rain, and it did not rain on the land for three and a half years. Again he prayed, and the heavens gave rain, and the earth produced its crops."

James 5:13–18

Yet another suggestion I want to make in relation to this matter of intercession is this—invite God to lay a need upon your heart. God does nothing without our consent and cooperation, so He needs our willingness before He will put some spiritual concern upon our hearts. But how does God lay a need upon the heart? That is a question to which we must address ourselves now. Some needs are obvious, and we don't need God to put them on our hearts—needs, for example, such as our families, our friends, the spiritual awakening of our community or church, and so on. But there are other needs, special needs, that God wants to share with us so that we in turn may bring them before Him in believing prayer.

Kindled Compassion

We will know when God lays a special concern on our hearts: it is when we feel something kindle within us at the news of someone's great need or some cause languishing for the want of spiritual help. This "kindling" I am talking about is something more than a human response; it is a mingling of the human and the divine. When God lays a need on our hearts, the matter does not simply take hold of us—it controls us. It burns its way to the very center of our being. Then the pity, the compassion, the love, and the purity of God ache inside us, and we cry out to help.

We help as we give ourselves to prayer. It may be, of course, that we can help in other ways, such as giving or service, but we help most by deep and intensive prayer. The intercessor opens up the conduits of spiritual power and provides dynamite where the work was previoiusly being done with picks and shovels. I say again, nothing is as powerful and as mighty as firm, confident, persevering, intercessory prayer. Nothing!

O Father, once again I open up my heart to You so that Your love, Your pity, and Your compassion may ache in me. I know that, properly employed, nothing is as mighty as prayer. Keep that conviction always growing within me. In Jesus' Name. Amen.

THE INTERCESSOR OPENS UP THE
CONDUITS OF SPIRITUAL POWER.

"ALL THINGS SERVE"

"And this is my prayer: that your love may abound more and more in knowledge and depth of insight, so that you may be able to discern what is best and may be pure and blameless until the day of Christ, filled with the fruit of righteousness that comes through Jesus Christ—to the glory and praise of God. Now I want you to know, brothers, that what has happened to me has really served to advance the gospel. As a result, it has become clear throughout the whole palace guard and to everyone else that I am in chains for Christ. Because of my chains, most of the brothers in the Lord have been encouraged to speak the word of God more courageously and fearlessly."

Philippians 1:9–14

One of the problems about which people often talk to me in connection with prayer is the problem of wandering thoughts. Mind wandering makes it hard to achieve that vivid awareness of God that is so essential to intercession. Even those who are well advanced in the school of intercession can be attacked in this way. Here is my suggestion on how to deal with this problem: if your mind wanders, do not despair—pray for the thing to which your mind has wandered. In that way you can redeem the wandering—it will be prayerful wandering.

Dealing with Distractions

A lady once said to me, "Whenever I begin to pray, I find that anything can then distract me—the slightest noise in the house, the siren of an ambulance or a police car—and I find it difficult to pull my thoughts back again." I suggested that when that happened, she focus on how to use distractions rather than allow them to defeat her prayer life. "But how?" she asked. "Take the ambulance or police siren," I said. "The next time you hear that, pray something like this: 'O Lord, this siren is distracting me, but I realize it is just a warning for people to move out of the way so that the police or the ambulance might come more speedily to someone's aid. Be with the person whom they are trying to help. If that person is not a Christian, draw him or her to Yourself, and help in the hour of need.'" Months later this lady told me that these simple words of advice had transformed her prayer time.

You need not worry about mind wandering if you make it a prayerful wandering. Then the distraction becomes a direction. "All things serve."

Father, help me use this technique the next time I am afflicted with a wandering thought. Help me see that I can turn even this difficulty into a door—a door that opens out to You. In Jesus' Name I ask it. Amen.

PRAY FOR THE THING TO WHICH YOUR
MIND HAS WANDERED.

GIVE GOD A MOMENT

"Then Jesus went with his disciples to a place called Gethsemane, and he said to them, 'Sit here while I go over there and pray.' He took Peter and the two sons of Zebedee along with him, and he began to be sorrowful and troubled. Then he said to them, 'My soul is overwhelmed with sorrow to the point of death. Stay here and keep watch with me.' Going a little farther, he fell with his face to the ground and prayed, 'My Father, if it is possible, may this cup be taken from me. Yet not as I will, but as you will.' Then he returned to his disciples and found them sleeping. 'Could you men not keep watch with me for one hour?' he asked Peter. 'Watch and pray so that you will not fall into temptation. The spirit is willing, but the body is weak.'"

Matthew 26:36–41

Today we bring to a close our meditations on the theme of prayer. Permit me to remind you of what I said earlier—that for the most part the suggestions I have given on building an effective prayer life are merely the scaffolding which can be taken down when the building is intact. Build into your life the habit of prayer, and increasingly the desire to pray will possess you. Then the busiest day will seem a day ill-spent unless it has included some time given to prayer.

Of Lasting Value

A few who have followed these meditations—the retired, the shut-ins, and those with few earthly responsibilities—may feel the call to make prayer their main ministry and join the thin ranks of the intercessors. I sincerely hope so. But whether it is one's main ministry or not, everyone who is in Christ can and ought to pray. In heaven we will find that nothing we did on earth was as lasting or as influential as prayer.

I will end with the famous parable of Tagore, the Indian poet. "I had gone a begging from door to door in the village path when a golden chariot appeared in the distance. It was the King of kings. The chariot stopped where I stood and the Master's glance fell on me. The Master held out His hand and said, 'What have you to give to me?' I took from my pocket the least little grain of corn and gave it to Him. How great was my surprise at the end of the day when I emptied my bag on the floor and there found a little grain of gold among the poor heap. I wept bitterly and wished that I had given him more."

The message is clear—give God a moment and He will turn it to gold. Give Him an hour—what then?

Father, I have been exposed to the theory
of prayer—now for the practice. Take me on from
here to experience and enjoy a more powerful
prayer life than I have ever known before.
In Jesus' Name I ask it. Amen.

BUILD INTO YOUR LIFE THE HABIT OF PRAYER.

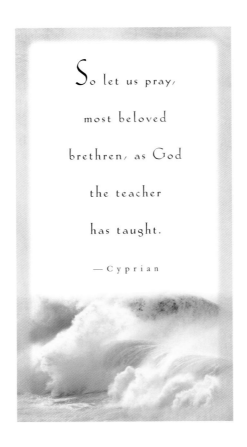

So let us pray,

most beloved

brethren, as God

the teacher

has taught.

— Cyprian

AUSTRALIA: CMC Australasia
P.O. Box 519, Belmont, Victoria 3216 Tel: (03) 5241 3288

CANADA: CMC Distribution Ltd.
P.O. Box 7000, Niagara on the Lake, Ontario L0S 1J0 Tel: 1 800 325 1297

INDIA: Full Gospel Literature Stores
254 Kilpauk Garden Road, Chennai 600010 Tel: (44) 644 3073

KENYA: Keswick Bookshop
P.O. Box 10242, Nairobi Tel: (02) 331692/226047

MALAYSIA: Salvation Book Centre (M)
23 Jalan SS2/64, Sea Park, 47300 Petaling Jaya, Selangor Tel: (3) 7766411

NEW ZEALAND: CMC New Zealand Ltd.
P.O. Box 949, 205 King Street South, Hastings
Tel: (6) 8784408, Toll free: 0800 333639

NIGERIA: FBFM (Every Day with Jesus)
Prince's Court, 37 Ahmed Onibudo Street, P.O. Box 70952, Victoria Island
Tel: 01 2617721, 616832, 4700218

REPUBLIC OF IRELAND: Scripture Union
40 Talbot Street, Dublin 1 Tel: (01) 8363764

SINGAPORE: Campus Crusade Asia Ltd.
315 Outram Road, 06–08 Tan Boon Liat Building, Singapore 169074
Tel: (65) 222 3640

SOUTH AFRICA: Struik Christian Books (Pty Ltd)
P.O. Box 193, Maitland 7405, Cape Town Tel: (021) 551 5900

SRI LANKA: Christombu Investments
27 Hospital Street, Colombo 1 Tel: (1) 433142/328909

USA: CMC Distribution
P.O. Box 644, Lewiston, New York 14092–0644 Tel: 1 800 325 1297